PRAYING
YOUR WAY
TO A
Blessed
Life

PRAYING YOUR WAY TO A

Blessed Life

DAILY PRAYERS FOR WOMEN

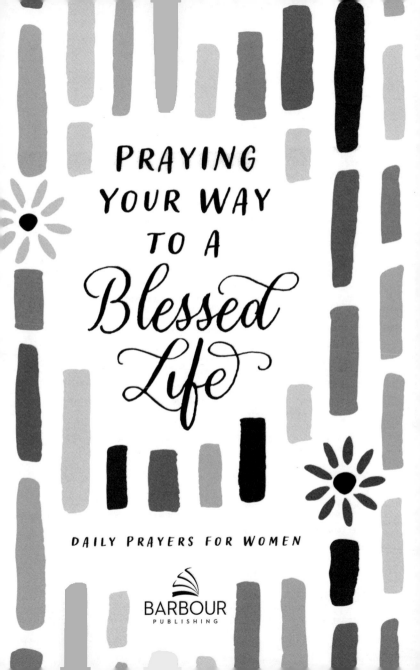

BARBOUR
PUBLISHING

INTRODUCTION

If you crave a life overflowing with God's blessings. . .
this book of daily prayers is just what your heart needs!

This book of daily inspirational prayers will set you on a path to blessed living. Each devotional-like prayer and related scripture selection will help you discover peace and comfort, delight and contentment, compassion and grace, and so much more every day of the year! Between the pages of this book, you'll embrace a life overflowing with the goodness of God.

A truly blessed life. . .is just a prayer away!

Day 1
DIPPING INTO GOD'S STRENGTH

*They read from the book of the Law of God, telling the
meaning of it so that they understood what was read. . . .
Ezra said to them, "Go, eat and drink what you enjoy, and give
some to him who has nothing ready. For this day is holy to our
Lord. Do not be sad for the joy of the Lord is your strength."*
NEHEMIAH 8:8, 10 NLV

Lord, so many times I find myself trying to live in my own
strength, and by the end of the day, I come up empty and sad,
tired and worn. Yet when I see this passage in Your Book, I realize I've been drawing from the wrong well. So here I am, Lord,
coming to You, finding where my true strength lies—in Your joy.
I am dipping into Your love, communing with Your Spirit, filling
up on the sheer bliss of Your presence. Be with me here and now
and throughout this day as I feast on You, share Your blessings
with others, and discover Your everlasting joy. Amen.

Day 2

SEEING CLEARLY

When I became a man, I put the ways of childhood behind me. For now we see only a reflection as in a mirror; then we shall see face to face. Now I know in part; then I shall know fully, even as I am fully known. And now these three remain: faith, hope and love. But the greatest of these is love.

1 Corinthians 13:11–13

Lord, I have gazed into antique mirrors. It's difficult to make out my features through the marred surface and dim reflection. I have to remind myself that this is also how I see You—through the limited lens of my humanity. I can just trace the outline of Your features but not quite see the fullness of Your glory. But I have the hope that one day I will see You face-to-face! I will know You as You so completely know every facet of who I am. For now I trust the shadow of You that I can see and the image of You that is etched in Your Word, but I also long for the day when I will know You more. In Jesus' name, amen.

Day 3

TRUSTING CONFIDENCE

*Thus said the Lord God, the Holy One of Israel:
In returning [to Me] and resting [in Me] you shall be
saved; in quietness and in [trusting] confidence shall
be your strength. . . . And your ears will hear a word
behind you, saying, This is the way; walk in it, when you
turn to the right hand and when you turn to the left.*
ISAIAH 30:15, 21 AMPC

These words are a reminder to me, Lord, of what I need to do, what I *want* to do, to have a good and peaceable life. I'm to return to You, to depend on You alone—not on fellow humans, animals, or machines. Only then will I find the true rest I need each day. Only then will my spirit find the quietness that feeds it, my soul the trusting confidence that nourishes it. As I rest and replenish myself in You, I find the strength to do what You've created me to do, to be who You created me to be. As I walk, Lord, direct my feet. Open my ears to Your Spirit's guidance every step of the way. Amen.

Day 4

ALL GOOD THINGS

Keep me, O God, for I am safe in You. I said to the Lord, "You are my Lord. All the good things I have come from You." As for those in the land who belong to You, they are the great ones in whom is all my joy.
PSALM 16:1–3 NLV

Lord, when I am alone, scared, or confused, I know I can run to You. You are the one who can protect me from all that comes against me, within and without. In You I can hide from the lure of the world. In You my soul and spirit find peace and calm. You have a way of unruffling my feathers ever so gently. So now, in this moment, I come to rest in Your companionable light, love, and silence. Place Your hedge of protection around me, sheltering me from outside dangers and inner negative thoughts. Remind me that all the good I have in this life comes from You. Thank You, Lord, for all Your blessings upon me and for all the joy You have waiting for me as I wait on You. "You are my Lord. All the good things I have come from You." In Jesus' name, I pray, amen.

Day 5
DOOR OF HOPE

"But then I will win her back once again. I will lead her
into the desert and speak tenderly to her there. I will
return her vineyards to her and transform the Valley
of Trouble into a gateway of hope. She will give herself
to me there, as she did long ago when she was young,
when I freed her from her captivity in Egypt."
HOSEA 2:14–15 NLT

God, I have stumbled through deep hollows—shadowed and chilly places unreached by the sun. I have known trouble and hardship and heartbreak. Life hasn't always treated me with gentle hands. And I've run from You. But I cling to this promise: You can transform valleys of trouble into doors of hope. You came to bind up the brokenhearted and set captives free, Jesus. I have been a prisoner of my own despair, but no more! I'm leaving my chains and walking through the door of Your hope into freedom. You have wooed me with Your love, compassion, and faithfulness. I don't deserve Your attentiveness, Lord, but You've remained devoted to me despite of my failures. In the beautiful name of Jesus, amen.

Day 6

LIFE—BREATHING THOUGHTS

Finally, brothers and sisters, whatever is true, whatever is noble, whatever is right, whatever is pure, whatever is lovely, whatever is admirable—if anything is excellent or praiseworthy—think about such things. Whatever you have learned or received or heard from me, or seen in me—put it into practice. And the God of peace will be with you.
PHILIPPIANS 4:8–9

God, as I listen to the negative self-chatter filling my mind, I realize these lies are not of You. These critical expectations and shame-filled words are taking up space where You long to breathe unconditional love and gentle words. Do You see the ways I'm so hard on myself? The stories I make up and the shame I readily dump on my good intentions? I'd never speak to my kids or friends this way, and therefore, I want to be gracious with myself as well.

Forgive me, Father. Please replace self-loathing thoughts with thoughts that are beautiful and true and saturated in self-control, thoughts that breathe life and declutter the lies. Spirit, please redirect my negative self-talk with whatever is pure and lovely and true so that I may go about my day open to Your truths and with space to receive. Amen.

Day 7

TRANQUILITY OF HEART AND LIFE

*And the Lord said to Moses, Say to Aaron and his sons,
This is the way you shall bless the Israelites. Say to them,
The Lord bless you and watch, guard, and keep you; the
Lord make His face to shine upon and enlighten you and
be gracious (kind, merciful, and giving favor) to you; the
Lord lift up His [approving] countenance upon you and
give you peace (tranquility of heart and life continually).*
NUMBERS 6:22–26 AMPC

I am so ready for peace, Lord. I'm tired of losing my cool, of letting my emotions take over. So help me get it through my head, Lord, that You are continually blessing me. That You are guarding and taking care of me no matter where I am or what I'm doing. That Your face shines on me, if only I would just look up and search for it. That You are kindness itself and overflow with mercy. And that best of all, You are continually giving me the peace that I crave, calming my heart and my life. All I have to do is receive it. And that's what I do in this moment, Lord, as I open my heart and mind to You. Flood me with Your peace. Amen.

Day 8

HAPPINESS FOREVER

My future is in Your hands. The land given to me is good. Yes, my share is beautiful to me. . . . For You will not give me over to the grave. And You will not allow Your Holy One to return to dust. You will show me the way of life. Being with You is to be full of joy. In Your right hand there is happiness forever.
PSALM 16:5–6, 10–11 NLV

Lord, when I'm stuck in a pattern of negative thoughts or am allowing fear to control my life, my heart races, my brow sweats, my soul despairs, and my spirit sinks. And it's all because I've somehow moved away from You and forgotten Your power, grace, mercy, strength, and help. I'm allowing everything *but You* to control me. So I'm back, Lord, remembering *You* are the one who holds my future. *You* are the one who helped me in the past and has given me all the good I have. So here I am in the present in Your presence. Here with You I find my joy! For I know You will show me the way You would have me go, the way that leads to that happily forever after. Amen.

Day 9
MY ANCHOR

*So God has given both his promise and his oath. These
two things are unchangeable because it is impossible for
God to lie. Therefore, we who have fled to him for refuge
can have great confidence as we hold to the hope that lies
before us. This hope is a strong and trustworthy anchor
for our souls. It leads us through the curtain into God's
inner sanctuary. Jesus has already gone in there for us.*
HEBREWS 6:18–20 NLT

God, You are the promise keeper and the hope giver. Your promises give flight to my hope, and it soars high on confident wings because I know that You can't lie. Everything You have said will happen just as You've planned. Just as Abraham patiently waited for his promised rewards, we will wait patiently, knowing that You keep Your promises to us. Instead of drifting on a sea of fear and uncertainty, I have moored myself to the anchor of hope in You. I can come directly to Your throne, God, because Jesus made it possible. And He intercedes for me. Even when I'm not sure what I need to pray, Your Holy Spirit has the words I lack. In the name of Your precious Son, Jesus, amen.

Day 10

UNBROKEN COMPANIONSHIP

*The Lord [earnestly] waits [expecting, looking, and
longing] to be gracious to you; and therefore He lifts
Himself up, that He may have mercy on you and show
loving-kindness to you. For the Lord is a God of justice.
Blessed (happy, fortunate, to be envied) are all those who
[earnestly] wait for Him, who expect and look and long
for Him [for His victory, His favor, His love, His peace,
His joy, and His matchless, unbroken companionship]!*
ISAIAH 30:18 AMPC

How wondrous is Your love for me, Lord. To think that You are
longing to be gracious to me. That You, the Creator and Sustainer
of the universe, are rising up to show me the mercy and compassion You have for me. As You look down, waiting for me, I'm
looking up to You. I am patiently waiting, expecting and longing
for You and all the blessings You have in store for me. You have
perfect timing, Lord. You know just what to do and when to do
it. So I'm leaning back on You, fully confident in Your goodness
and basking in Your presence, loving Your peace and this sense
of unbroken companionship with and in You. Amen.

Day 11

A RESTART

A hot-tempered person stirs up conflict,
but the one who is patient calms a quarrel.
PROVERBS 15:18

Lord, today my patience well is dry. I'm frustrated with my kids, my temper is short, and I admit that I'm not momming well. In fact, I'd like to relieve myself of mom duties at the moment and crawl back into bed. Thank You for hearing me and understanding as a parent Yourself. God, where criticism is at an all-time high, would You replace that with compassion? Where anger comes in a raised voice, would You replace it with a gentle response? God, I need a deep breath, a restart. Would You help me see my children's hearts with Your lens—beyond their behavior and straight into their souls? May I scoop them up and whisper sincere love and affirmations over them. And would You do the same for me, my gentle, loving Father, in the moments when I'm quick to beat myself up? After all, I am Your kid too, and sometimes I just need a heavenly hug. Amen.

Day 12

KEEP ASKING, SEEKING, AND KNOCKING

Keep on asking and it will be given you; keep on seeking and you will find; keep on knocking [reverently] and [the door] will be opened to you. For everyone who keeps on asking receives; and he who keeps on seeking finds; and to him who keeps on knocking, [the door] will be opened.
MATTHEW 7:7–8 AMPC

Just when I'm ready to give up, Lord, You bring scriptures like this to my attention and give me the hope I need to keep coming to You. Through Your Son, Jesus, You've made it clear that if I keep asking, seeking, and knocking, You *will* come through for me. I *will* receive what I'm asking for, find what I seek, and have doors opened to me. So here I am, Lord, asking, seeking, and knocking, knowing You will provide what I desire. And if need be, You'll change that desire to better align with Yours. In this and so many other ways, Lord, You revive my hope. Joy begins to warm my heart as my discouragement morphs into encouragement. Thank You for all this and more. I pray in Jesus' name, amen.

Day 13

SWEET WISDOM

*My child, eat honey, for it is good, and the honeycomb
is sweet to the taste. In the same way, wisdom is
sweet to your soul. If you find it, you will have a bright
future, and your hopes will not be cut short.*
PROVERBS 24:13–14 NLT

Heavenly Father, the world markets its own brand of wisdom
and understanding, and it can be persuasive and appear logical.
But Your Word says that the fear of the Lord is the beginning of
wisdom. Father, I want to honor You with my life and walk in wisdom as a daughter of the King. I want that bright and hope-filled
future that You offer to all who are guided by Your wise counsel. My soul craves the truth of Your Word, and it delights my
tongue like a decadent chocolate dessert dripping with warm
fudge. Teach me to seek Your wisdom and direct my decisions,
for I know my hopes will not be disappointed in You. In Jesus'
name, amen.

Day 14
THE PEACE OF ME

*"This book of instruction must not depart from your mouth;
you are to recite it day and night so that you may carefully
observe everything written in it. For then you will prosper
and succeed in whatever you do. Haven't I commanded you:
be strong and courageous? Do not be afraid or discouraged,
for the LORD your God is with you wherever you go."*
JOSHUA 1:8–9 HCSB

Throughout Your Word, Lord, You continually tell me to be
strong and courageous. It's not just an idea or a polite request—
You *command* this of me! So why is it sometimes so hard to do?
Why do I too often feel weak and frightened? To grasp on to or
lay claim to this strength and courage You offer, help me, Lord,
to go deeper into this command. To meditate on it, memorize
it, and melt it into my heart. Then once strength and courage
become the very fabric of my being, lead me to the next words
You would have me learn and memorize, until they fill me with
peace. In Jesus' name, amen.

Day 15

TRADING COMPARISON FOR CONTENTMENT

"If God so clothes the grass, which is alive in the field today, and tomorrow is thrown into the oven, how much more will he clothe you, O you of little faith! . . . All the nations of the world seek after these things, and your Father knows that you need them. Instead, seek his kingdom, and these things will be added to you."
LUKE 12:28, 30–31 ESV

Okay, God, I'm finding myself looking around and comparing. *They get to go on vacation. Their marriage looks perfect. I bet their kids are always respectful. Oh look, they're remodeling their kitchen.*

Jealousy.

I'm embarrassed, but this is my true heart. Would You please forgive me? God, You are taking care of me. You care about feeding birds and clothing wildflowers; help me trust that You are giving me more than I need.

Please replace my comparison with a content heart. One that is thankful and quick to give You praise for what *is* happening, what *is* my reality: a heartbeat, health, this roof above my head. Give me thankful awareness for the clothes I wear, the people that come across my path, and this life that's a gift. In You, my soul finds contentment. Amen.

Day 16

GIVING WAY TO GOD

Do not trouble yourself because of sinful men. Do not want to be like those who do wrong. For they will soon dry up like the grass. Like the green plant they will soon die. Trust in the Lord, and do good. So you will live in the land and will be fed. Be happy in the Lord. And He will give you the desires of your heart. Give your way over to the Lord. Trust in Him also. And He will do it.
PSALM 37:1–5 NLV

Lord, through Your Word, You have given me the way to walk the road of joy. First, I'm not to worry about those who are divisive or seem intent on doing evil. They will not be around forever. Instead, I'm to trust in You and do good in this world. Then I will find all I need to live the life You have designed for me. Then I will find all the joy in You and receive the desires of my heart. So in this moment, right here, right now, I'm letting You take control of my life. I'm trusting You for all, knowing it is in You alone I'll find joy. Amen.

Day 17

WINGS OF HOPE

[The Lord] never grows weak or weary. No one can measure the depths of his understanding. He gives power to the weak and strength to the powerless. Even youths will become weak and tired, and young men will fall in exhaustion. But those who trust in the Lord will find new strength. They will soar high on wings like eagles. They will run and not grow weary. They will walk and not faint.

Isaiah 40:28–31 NLT

Lord, I'm exhausted by the struggle of this world. I've been trying to do it all on my own. And I've been failing miserably. I'm driven to my knees by weakness. I was about to collapse in hopeless despair, but then I looked up to heaven and I found You. The tireless Creator. The strength giver. Lord God, I trust You. I trust Your understanding of every impossible and strength-sapping situation I'll ever encounter, and I give them to You. I'm off-loading my stress onto the wide span of Your strong shoulders. I can do nothing without You. Pour new strength into my weary body. I want to soar like the eagles and work in Your kingdom zealously. In Jesus' name, amen.

Day 18

HEART POUR, PEACE RICH

Hannah said, "Oh no, sir—please! I'm a woman brokenhearted. . . . The only thing I've been pouring out is my heart, pouring it out to GOD. . . . It's because I'm so desperately unhappy and in such pain that I've stayed here so long." Eli answered her, "Go in peace. And may the God of Israel give you what you have asked of him.". . . She. . .went her way. Then she ate heartily, her face radiant.

1 SAMUEL 1:15–18 MSG

Overwhelmed, I come to You, Lord. I've been picked on, bullied, taunted, teased, and trampled. No one understands the pain I'm feeling except for You. So it's to You I come. It's to You that I pour out my troubles, bare my soul, and bring my heartfelt desires. It is before You that I get the relief I so crave. It's from You that I receive the peace I need to rise up from my knees and carry on. May You, Lord, my God, my beloved, my prince, grant me what I have asked for, what I long for. Be with me as I go on my way in You, heart no longer heavy but filled with peace. In Jesus' name, amen.

Day 19

THANKS IN THE EVERYDAYNESS

*Whatever you do, work at it with all your heart,
as working for the Lord, not for human masters, since
you know that you will receive an inheritance from the
Lord as a reward. It is the Lord Christ you are serving.*
COLOSSIANS 3:23–24

God, I admit, as I'm washing dishes, that I forget to thank You for the everyday provisions like plates and forks and food. How much I have to be thankful for and how often I neglect to pause and thank You first for the miraculously minuscule ways You show up—in weekday dinners and dirty silverware. These reminders are Your invitation for coming together, eating with neighbors, and enjoying recipes together. The dish washing is the celebration for a meal well spent, conversations well shared. Plates and forks joyfully messed. Forgive me for complaining instead of rejoicing. Turn my heart now toward praise. Yay for dirty dishes, for each one signifies a person fed nourishment and soul care in my home. May You be the center of every meal and conversation from this day forward. In Jesus' name, amen.

Day 20
GREAT EXPECTATIONS

*The Lord [earnestly] waits [expecting, looking, and longing]
to be gracious to you; and therefore He lifts Himself up,
that He may have mercy on you and show loving-kindness
to you. . . . Blessed (happy, fortunate, to be envied) are all
those who [earnestly] wait for Him, who expect and look and
long for Him [for His victory, His favor, His love, His peace,
His joy, and His matchless, unbroken companionship]!*
ISAIAH 30:18 AMPC

How wonderful, Lord, that in every moment You are waiting
and expecting to be gracious to me. You have scads of mercy
and loving-kindness whenever I need it. So help me be patient,
Lord. Help me to drop whatever burdens I'm bearing and open
my arms to You and the blessings You have for me. My eyes are
on You. I long for Your never-ending supply of strength, love,
peace, and joy. I cherish and seek Your company, Your "matchless, unbroken companionship," each and every second of my
day. For I know that by returning and resting in You, I will be
saved. In quietness and trusting confidence, I will find my source
of strength (see Isaiah 30:15). Amen.

Day 21

DELIGHTED TO KNOW ME

*The LORD, the King of Israel, is with you; never again will
you fear any harm. On that day they will say to Jerusalem,
"Do not fear, Zion; do not let your hands hang limp.
The LORD your God is with you, the Mighty Warrior who
saves. He will take great delight in you; in his love he will no
longer rebuke you, but will rejoice over you with singing."*
ZEPHANIAH 3:15–17

Lord, I feel disliked and unaccepted. Does anyone cherish my
friendship or the person that You made me to be? The enemy
tells me I'm overlooked and unappreciated by everyone. But,
Father, Your Word says something different. It tells me something bright and encouraging. Even if every person on this earth
is ambivalent to my presence here, You take great delight in me.
You cherish me and rejoice over me. You're so happy to see
me that You sing with joy when I enter Your courts. Because
You formed every cell of my being and molded every facet of
my personality, You think I'm the best thing You've ever done!
Thank You for loving me. In the name of Your Son, Jesus, amen.

Day 22

A PICTURE OF PEACE

Like an apple tree among the trees of the wood, so is my beloved [shepherd] among the sons [cried the girl]! . . . [I can feel] his left hand under my head and his right hand embraces me! . . . [Vividly she pictured it] The voice of my beloved [shepherd]! . . . Arise, my love, my fair one, and come away.
SONG OF SOLOMON 2:3, 6, 8, 13 AMPC

You, Lord, are my pathway to peace. I look to You. I picture You lying beside me. When I close my eyes and imagine You here with me, I can feel Your left hand under my head, Your right hand embracing me, pulling me close to Your warmth and love, giving me the comfort I long for. And as I lie here, totally content, amazingly calm, I know nothing can harm me. Nothing can worry or dismay me. For not only do I feel Your presence but hear Your voice telling me You love me. That You will continually protect and guide me. That because of You in my life, I need not complain, worry, or fear. Thank You, Lord, for this picture of peace. Amen.

Day 23
KINGDOM PERSPECTIVE

*He told them another parable: "The kingdom of heaven
is like a mustard seed, which a man took and planted in
his field. Though it is the smallest of all seeds, yet when
it grows, it is the largest of garden plants and becomes a
tree, so that the birds come and perch in its branches."*
MATTHEW 13:31–32

God, You say the kingdom is like a mustard seed, and mustard seeds are small. How often do I think of the word *kingdom* and imagine big, flashy, and powerful? To You, kingdom perspective is about the heart. Forgive me for getting caught up in the world's perspective of kingdom instead of Your eternal kingdom. Stir me toward grand in Your eyes—small as a mustard seed. This is my goal.

Whisper Your delight in me as I go about the small tasks of my day. Please remind me that these mustard-seed miracles are building "the largest of plants," where shade and refuge will be available to others. I desire to have a heart that follows Your lead, regardless of outcome or status. Your kingdom is coming, and what matters most is my eternal deposits I'm making on earth: You and people. This is enough. In Jesus' name, amen.

Day 24
MORE THAN YOU NEED

Do not trouble yourself when all goes well with the one who carries out his sinful plans. Stop being angry. Turn away from fighting. Do not trouble yourself. It leads only to wrong-doing. For those who do wrong will be cut off. But those who wait for the Lord will be given the earth. . . . And they will be happy and have much more than they need.
Psalm 37:7–9, 11 NLV

Sometimes, Lord, I get so discouraged. It seems as if the people who get all the breaks are those who are *not* followers of You! It's so frustrating. But then I remember that even those who seem to have everything actually have nothing—because they don't have You. So I'm not going to worry about the ne'er-do-wells. Instead, I'm going to focus my eyes on You. I'm going to do good because I know it not only pleases You but also gives me so much joy. I'm waiting on You, Lord, following You, loving You, looking to You for everything. For when I give You my all, I get Your all. Amen.

Day 25
ALL I NEED

The LORD is my shepherd; I have all that I need. He lets me rest in green meadows; he leads me beside peaceful streams. He renews my strength. He guides me along right paths, bringing honor to his name. Even when I walk through the darkest valley, I will not be afraid, for you are close beside me. Your rod and your staff protect and comfort me.
PSALM 23:1–4 NLT

God, we're so unsatisfied and greedy. More stuff, bigger houses, better-paying jobs, luxurious vacations—we just want more. It's all too tempting to get whirled up into the cyclone of more. I think, *If I just made a few hundred dollars more every month, I'd be happy. If my house was remodeled, I'd be happy.* But would I? This hungry beast is never satisfied and leaves a wake of torn-up lives and brokenness behind. Father, instead of insatiable desires, You offer me contentment and rest. My every need is met in You. I realize that I have been seeking fulfillment but pursuing emptiness. But I've found the shepherd of my soul. Thank You, God, that You are all I've ever needed. Amen.

Day 26

MY BELOVED SHEPHERD

*[So I went with him, and when we were climbing the rocky
steps up the hillside, my beloved shepherd said to me] O my
dove, [while you are here]. . .in the sheltered and secret place
of the cliff, let me see your face, let me hear your voice;
for your voice is sweet, and your face is lovely. [My heart was
touched and I fervently sang to him my desire] Take for us the
foxes, the little foxes that spoil the vineyards [of our love].*
SONG OF SOLOMON 2:14–15 AMPC

In Your company, my beloved, I can climb to the highest of
heights. You keep me safe and secluded in Your secret place.
It's here You ask me to let You see my face and hear my voice.
Just the fact that You'd like to do those things, to listen to me
and love me, brings me so much joy. So I am ready to raise my
voice to You in song, Lord. Allow me to stay in You, walk with
You, climb with You. And to rest in You, confident You will remove anything that threatens to come between us. In Jesus'
name, amen.

Day 27

THE SHEER BEAUTY OF CREATING

*"He has filled them with skill to do all kinds of work
as engravers, designers, embroiderers in blue, purple
and scarlet yarn and fine linen, and weavers—
all of them skilled workers and designers."*
EXODUS 35:35

I am made in the image of the mighty Creator and therefore am creative. God, awaken me to the ways that You made me to feel alive while creating. Is it picking wildflowers and pressing them between book pages to make art? Is it baking cookies for the neighborhood kids? Is it singing? Writing? Quilting? Whatever the creative magic You sewed into me since before time, pull that out of me today. Help me delight in creating for the sheer beauty of creating—not the final result, but the joy in the creative process. Forgive me when I forget that this spark You've given me is unique; no one else has the same way of creating from my perspective. Help me not squander but generously use my gift. I'm so thankful I have a Father who enjoys making and creating and living in this creative space. In Jesus' name, amen.

Day 28
A SAFE PLACE

The steps of a good man are led by the Lord. And He is happy in his way. When he falls, he will not be thrown down, because the Lord holds his hand. . . . For the Lord loves what is fair and right. He does not leave the people alone who belong to Him. . . . He. . .saves them, because they go to Him for a safe place.
PSALM 37:23–24, 28, 40 NLV

Here's one of the things I love most about You, Lord. When I follow Your way instead of my own, I am happy, full of that inner joy only You can supply, no matter what happens. Because even if I trip up, You come to my rescue. You hold my hand and pull me back up on my feet so I can start all over again. As I grow closer and closer to You, I know I'm exactly where I belong. For You promise to always be with me. You will never leave me alone because I am Your daughter, precious in Your sight. And when things go dark, when shadows chase me, I run to You, straight into Your arms, where I am not only safe but comforted and remade. Amen.

Day 29
INTERCESSOR

The Holy Spirit prays for us with groanings that cannot be expressed in words. And the Father who knows all hearts knows what the Spirit is saying, for the Spirit pleads for us believers in harmony with God's own will. And we know that God causes everything to work together for the good of those who love God and are called according to his purpose for them.
ROMANS 8:26–28 NLT

Lord, I don't pretend to understand Your will in every situation. Often I don't even know which outcome to pray for. I know what I want in the moment, but I'm blinded by my shortsighted-ness. It's a great relief to know that You see the endgame, and You've given me Your Holy Spirit to pray for me when I have no words. You work every circumstance for the good of Your king-dom and Your children who love You. I may suffer here, but You don't waste a single moment of my life. Instead You use them to make me more like Jesus. Thank You for refining me into a useful instrument. Smooth away my ragged edges so I can be used by You. Amen.

Day 30
A GREAT AND WONDERFUL CALM

They. . .awakened Him, saying, Lord, rescue and preserve us!
We are perishing! And He said to them, Why are you timid
and afraid, O you of little faith? Then He got up and rebuked
the winds and the sea, and there was a great and wonderful
calm (a perfect peaceableness). And the men were stunned
with bewildered wonder and marveled, saying, What kind
of Man is this, that even the winds and the sea obey Him!
MATTHEW 8:25–27 AMPC

When I'm in the middle of a storm, Lord, I know that because of Your presence, because You are riding out the storm with me, I have nothing at all to worry about. I have nothing at all to fear. After all, You have already rescued me from death. You have already overcome all evil. So all I need to do is remain confident that You are in control of the situation. That You will, at just the right moment, rise up and tame the wind and waves assailing me. You will take this tumultuous situation and bring into it a great and wonderful calm. And I will once more stand before You and marvel. Amen.

Day 31

DELIGHTFUL CELEBRATION

*Rejoice in the Lord always. I will say it again: Rejoice!
Let your gentleness be evident to all. The Lord is near. Do not
be anxious about anything, but in every situation, by prayer
and petition, with thanksgiving, present your requests to God.
And the peace of God, which transcends all understanding,
will guard your hearts and your minds in Christ Jesus.*

PHILIPPIANS 4:4–7

God, I find it easy to celebrate when life is going as planned, when circumstances are favorable and comfortable. Yet, I know You do Your greatest work in my discomfort. But for today, I will rejoice. I will tuck this moment away and pull it out for the hard days.

As Job said, we are so quick to praise in the good and complain in the hard. Forgive me, God, for treating You like a genie and questioning Your ways when life goes off course. Today, I will pull out the fancy china, sing in the car, and smile at every stranger. I will celebrate, for I am savoring every moment, every feeling, every creation sighting, and conversation. You are in all of this, and I give thanks to You and experience sheer and utter delight! Amen.

Day 32
A GRAND PLAN

*I know the thoughts and plans that I have for you,
says the Lord, thoughts and plans for welfare and peace
and not for evil, to give you hope in your final outcome.
Then you will call upon Me, and you will come and pray
to Me, and I will hear and heed you. Then you will seek
Me, inquire for, and require Me [as a vital necessity] and
find Me when you search for Me with all your heart.*
JEREMIAH 29:11–13 AMPC

I love that You have a plan for me, Lord. The fact that You even *think* of me is astounding! Sometimes I feel so lost in this world, as if I'm just one more bit of dust, unimportant, overlooked. And then I read in Your Word that if I call on You, You will bend Your ear to my lips. You'll actually *listen* to me, hear what I have to say, and move to work in my life. If I seek You with my whole self—my heart, soul, mind, and strength—and need You in every way, I *will* find You. All this is a balm for my soul and a joy to my spirit. Amen.

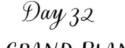

Day 33
I BELIEVE

It was not with perishable things such as silver or gold that you were redeemed from the empty way of life handed down to you from your ancestors, but with the precious blood of Christ, a lamb without blemish or defect. He was chosen before the creation of the world, but was revealed in these last times for your sake. Through him you believe in God, who raised him from the dead and glorified him, and so your faith and hope are in God.
1 PETER 1:18–21

God, I believe in You. I believe in Your love for me. And I believe that You sent Jesus to die for me. How awesome is Your love and wisdom, Father, that You chose Him for this purpose before You even spoke the first word of creation. I believe that You raised Him from the dead and that He is preparing my forever home with You for the day I will join You in eternity. My hope lives strong because I believe every word You have spoken. I experience Your love for me in the countless ways You provide for me, and I see it in Your exquisite care for my eternal soul. You didn't have to die, but You did. For me. Thank You, Jesus. Amen.

Day 34
"ALL IS WELL"

The child sat on her lap till noon, and then he died. And she went up and laid him on the bed of the man of God and shut the door behind him and went out. . . . She said, "All is well." . . . When the man of God saw her coming, he said to Gehazi his servant. . . "Run at once to meet her and say to her, 'Is all well with you? Is all well with your husband? Is all well with the child?' " And she answered, "All is well."
2 KINGS 4:20–21, 23, 25–26 ESV

There is something wonderful as well as disturbing in the story of the Shunammite woman, Lord. Even after her son dies, she keeps saying, "All is well." It's wonderful that she can remain that calm during such a heart-wrenching account. Yet at the same time, it's a bit disturbing that she does. What cool! What calm! Yet that's just the kind of peace I want, Lord. So help me to remember that with You living with me and in me, I too can have this woman's confidence. I too can have peace within even when it seems as if all is falling apart without. In Jesus' name, amen.

Day 35

A DEEP BREATH OF GRACE

For by grace you have been saved through faith.
And this is not your own doing; it is the gift of God,
not a result of works, so that no one may boast.
EPHESIANS 2:8–9 ESV

God, I'm noticing that my grace well is dry. I'm cranky and selfish, and life seems half-empty. Thank You for loving me as I am, but I know You desire more; You long for me to believe You saved me by Your grace, and because of this, I can fully offer grace to those around me. Offer me a deep breath of grace right now. I don't have to work for Your love—I'm covered. May this knowledge sink into my bones.

God, I want to be a soul who lavishes grace because I know of my need for Your grace first. Soak my soul in the gift of knowing You. As I spend time with You, may grace naturally overflow. A grace giver is who I want to be. Forgive me for expecting this gift when I'm quick to expect others to earn their favor from me. Grace upon grace upon grace is my prayer. In Jesus' name, amen.

Day 36
THE SECRET PLACE

The Lord is my light and the One Who saves me. Whom should I fear? The Lord is the strength of my life. Of whom should I be afraid? . . . In the day of trouble. . .In the secret place. . .He will hide me. He will set me high upon a rock. Then my head will be lifted up above all those around me who hate me. I will give gifts in His holy tent with a loud voice of joy.
PSALM 27:1, 5–6 NLV

Fear can be a major killjoy, but I'm shoring up my confidence in You, Lord. You are the most powerful being in heaven and on earth. So I need not fear anything or anyone who comes against me. You, Lord, are the one who gives me the strength to stand. My faith in You gives me the confidence I need. When the trouble starts, You give me shelter. You keep me from the darkness and warm me with Your light. When I'm in Your secret place, You increase my courage. And it is there that I cry out with joy, praising You with all my heart. Thank You, Lord, for being my all in all. Amen.

Day 37
THE NEW ME

*And he died for all, that those who live should no longer
live for themselves but for him who died for them and was
raised again. So from now on we regard no one from a
worldly point of view. Though we once regarded Christ in this
way, we do so no longer. Therefore, if anyone is in Christ,
the new creation has come: The old has gone, the new is here!*
2 CORINTHIANS 5:15–17

God, I thought there was no hope for me to ever be anything
different. I thought I could never climb out of the deep sludge
that filled the rut I was living in. I was convinced I wasn't worth
much. The world surely didn't see even a glimmer of potential
in me. But You did. You saw me as precious. You lifted me out
by a nail-marked hand and made me into something new. Praise
You, Jesus, the old, haggard me is gone. I'm different and better. It's me 2.0! Now I'm truly alive, and I spend my days living
for You because You died but live again. I was dead too—dead in
my sin and hopelessness—but no longer. In the saving name of
Jesus, amen.

Day 38
OPENED EYES

*An army with horses and chariots was around the city.
Elisha's servant said to him, Alas, my master! What shall
we do? [Elisha] answered, Fear not; for those with us are
more than those with them. Then Elisha prayed, Lord,
I pray You, open his eyes that he may see. And the Lord
opened the young man's eyes, and he saw, and behold,
the mountain was full of horses and chariots of fire.*
2 KINGS 6:15–17 AMPC

Lord, I feel like I'm surrounded by chaos. I'm overwhelmed, feeling hemmed in, as if there's no way out. That I have done all that I can do. But this is a battle I can no longer fight. So it is to You that I turn for help, for a solution, for hope. And as I turn my thoughts to You, as I lay my problem at Your feet, I hear Your voice, Your words telling me not to fear. You are more than able to protect me from all things, all people—even from my own self, doubts, and negative thoughts. You alone make it clear that I need never worry because there is no force more powerful than You. With opened eyes, I find my joy, my peace, my renewed hope and vision in You. Amen!

Day 39

TRUE COMFORT RESTORATION

*Your hands made me and formed me; give me understanding
to learn your commands. May those who fear you rejoice
when they see me, for I have put my hope in your word.
I know, LORD, that your laws are righteous, and that in
faithfulness you have afflicted me. May your unfailing love
be my comfort, according to your promise to your servant.*
PSALM 119:73–76

God, I hate being uncomfortable. I want to squirm free, push past this tension, and move on to the next comfortable thing.

I know staying in this space helps me depend on You for true comfort. Help me listen to my body and pay attention to when I'm uncomfortable and how I respond. How do I rush to squelch my anxiety? How are You inviting me to stay in this discomfort and why?

God, I acknowledge that when I'm uncomfortable, the ugliest parts come to the surface. As they do, would You please comfort me in my discomfort? Tether me close to Your Spirit so that when I'm anxious and scared and frantic to move from this space, I'll sense You drawing me to stay here and know what true comfort restoration looks like. In Jesus' name, amen.

Day 40
REQUEST GRANTED

Jabez was honorable above his brothers; but his mother named him Jabez [sorrow maker], saying, Because I bore him in pain. Jabez cried to the God of Israel, saying, Oh, that You would bless me and enlarge my border, and that Your hand might be with me, and You would keep me from evil so it might not hurt me! And God granted his request.
1 CHRONICLES 4:9–10 AMPC

I thank You, Lord, that You have provided me with the gift and tool of prayer. No matter how I am seen or labeled in this world, by praying to You, I can change the conversation within and without. Although my name is not sorrow maker, I ask You, Lord, for Your many blessings. I ask that You would increase what I already have. That Your hand would be with me to protect me. That You would keep me from evil so I am not hurt. That You would fill my head with good thoughts. That You would open my mind and heart to Your Word, allowing it to change me from the inside out for Your glory alone. In Jesus' name, I pray, amen.

Day 41
BIGGER PLANS

"You will conceive and give birth to a son, and you are to call him Jesus. He will be great and will be called the Son of the Most High. The Lord God will give him the throne of his father David, and he will reign over Jacob's descendants forever; his kingdom will never end."
Luke 1:31–33

Lord, Your plans are always far greater than anything I could imagine with my limited mental faculties. The Jewish people expected Your prophecies to be fulfilled by a mighty and powerful earthly king. They wanted a military and political victory over their oppressors. But instead You sent a baby to be born in a barn and heralded His coming to poor, outcast shepherds. And yet You gave us so much more than a king—You gave us a Savior. You gave us hope and love and relationship with You. You gave us mercy and grace and an everlasting kingdom that's not of this world. You gave us Jesus. Father, teach me to trust Your plans, because the nuances of Your design are fantastically beyond my wildest dreams. In Jesus' name, amen.

Day 42
BECAUSE OF YOU

*Standing behind Him at His feet weeping, she began to
wet His feet with [her] tears; and she wiped them with
the hair of her head and kissed His feet [affectionately]
and anointed them with the ointment (perfume). . . .
He said to her, Your sins are forgiven! . . . Your faith has
saved you; go (enter) into peace [in freedom from all the
distresses that are experienced as the result of sin].*
LUKE 7:38, 48, 50 AMPC

Jesus, You know I'm not perfect. Yet You still accept me, love
me, help me, and understand me when I come before You. If I
could, I would fall at Your feet, wet them with my tears of joy,
wipe them with my hair, anoint them with perfume, and cover
them in kisses. Because of You and what You did on the cross,
my sins have been forgiven and forgotten. Because of You, I can
come boldly before Father God and speak to Him. Because of
You, I can have peace of mind and freedom from stress. Because of You, I have a life I want to live and yet surrender to You.
What a God I serve! Amen!

Day 43
GIFT OF HEALTH

This was to fulfill what was spoken through the prophet
Isaiah: "He took up our infirmities and bore our diseases."
MATTHEW 8:17

My body aches, and I feel miserable. I don't have time to be sick. I'm humbled, God, because it's in my sickness that I am ever so aware of the many days I'm healthy. How quick I am to complain when I'm in bed but forget to praise You for the days I wake healthy and strong. I repent of this everyday miracle of health.

Health is a daily gift. Forgive me for taking this for granted. Today I will rest. I put on music and rest my body in soft sheets and pretend You are holding me while I'm ill. Use this ailment to deepen my dependency and to humble me more to Your Spirit. Awaken me to ways that the world goes on while I lie here resting. Invite me to further surrender my control and receive rest from You. Amen.

Day 44
STRENGTHENED WITH TRUST

The village. . .had been burned to the ground, and their wives, sons, and daughters all taken prisoner. David and his men burst out in loud wails—wept and wept until they were exhausted with weeping. . . . There was talk among the men, bitter over the loss of their families, of stoning him. David strengthened himself with trust in his GOD. . . . Then David prayed to GOD. . . . David recovered the whole lot.
1 SAMUEL 30:3–4, 6, 8, 19 MSG

Your Word makes clear, Lord, that there are times when it's okay to have a good cry. I should take time to mourn over the losses I suffer in this world. After all, Jesus cried, so why shouldn't I? Yet when I'm all cried out, I need to seek Your face so I can find my way out of any why-me conundrums. I garner strength and encouragement by sitting in Your presence. Then I am to pray, asking You what I should do to find a path to restoration. Only when I have received Your instruction am I to take the next steps. For only with Your power can I live out Your plan and be restored to joy once more. Amen.

Day 45
BORROWED RIGHTEOUSNESS

*But we who live by the Spirit eagerly wait to receive
by faith the righteousness God has promised to us.
For when we place our faith in Christ Jesus, there is no
benefit in being circumcised or being uncircumcised.
What is important is faith expressing itself in love.*
GALATIANS 5:5–6 NLT

God, I'm not good enough by myself. I'm unworthy, and I mess up more than I care to admit. And that's okay. Because I praise You, Jesus, that no amount of rule-following can make me truly righteous. I can't earn Your love through my actions and good deeds because You've already given it freely to me. I am made clean in Your eyes only through faith and the cleansing blood of Jesus. And while there's nothing wrong with doing good works for Your kingdom, what You require of Your followers is love. Lord, help me love better. My capacity for love often seems so limited compared to the unfathomable depth of Yours. Teach me to live in the Spirit and produce His fruits. Amen.

Day 46
THE SOUL CHILD WITHIN

Lord, my heart is not haughty, nor my eyes lofty; neither do I exercise myself in matters too great or in things too wonderful for me. Surely I have calmed and quieted my soul; like a weaned child with his mother, like a weaned child is my soul within me [ceased from fretting]. O Israel, hope in the Lord from this time forth and forever.

PSALM 131:1–3 AMPC

Father God, I have put aside any grandiose plans I may have had for myself. I don't get caught up in things that are way beyond my comprehension. Instead, I have put myself and my future in Your hands. I tackle the things You call me to do, follow the plans You have made for me, walk on the path You have laid out for me. I live and breathe in Your rhythm. In doing so, I have transformed my heart within to be calm. No outside or inside noises can shake me. I no longer fuss, fear, or fret. My soul is like a weaned child within me. I am in Your hands, held close with love because of Your Son, in whose name I pray. Amen.

Day 47
BEAUTY ALL AROUND

"Consider how the wild flowers grow. They do not labor or spin. Yet I tell you, not even Solomon in all his splendor was dressed like one of these."
LUKE 12:27

God, I look outside and see the vibrant green of grass and yellow flashes of wildflowers. Your beauty is everywhere, waiting to be enjoyed. Every delicate flower, the blue of the sky, the way the clouds form shapes and wisp across the horizon. . . Draw me to notice Your beauty in every person I interact with, the cup I drink from, and the architecture of buildings.

You waste nothing in design and structure and nature. Even when I cut an apple horizontally, there is Your beauty staring back in the form of a star. I'm aware of how often I take Your beauty for granted, for all of this—the beach, culture, various dialects, people, forests, and waves—is merely a facet of Your beauty.

God, how I want the earth's beauty to be an overarching imitation of the beauty You are. How I long to be in Your presence one day and to behold Your infinite beauty. Amen.

Day 48
NEVERTHELESS

*The king and his men went to Jerusalem against the
Jebusites, the inhabitants of the land, who said to David,
"You will not come in here, but the blind and the lame will
ward you off"—thinking, "David cannot come in here."
Nevertheless, David took the stronghold of Zion, that
is, the city of David. . . . And David became greater and
greater, for the Lord, the God of hosts, was with him.*
2 Samuel 5:6–7, 10 esv

Every success David had, Lord, was because You were with
him—*and* David was with You. That's how I want to live my life,
Lord. When You call me to do something, when You want me to
follow in Jesus' steps and to live out what You have planned for
me, I do not want to be dissuaded or discouraged by what other
people say. I want to *nevertheless* take the strongholds You want
me to take. Win the battles You want me to win. For then I will
have the joy of that success, and You will take joy in me as well.
Give me that courage, Lord. Be with me in all You would have
me do. Help me to live a nevertheless life for Your glory. Amen.

Day 49

A GOD WHO ANSWERS

*Those who would harm me talk of my ruin; all day long
they scheme and lie. I am like the deaf, who cannot hear,
like the mute, who cannot speak; I have become like
one who does not hear, whose mouth can offer no reply.
Lord, I wait for you; you will answer, Lord my God.*
PSALM 38:12–15

Heavenly Father, I plead to You in prayer day after day, and sometimes it seems the heavens echo back with deafening silence. I'm tempted to wonder if You're listening, if You care. But then I find promises in Your Word that sprout new hope in my heart like spring flowers unfurling their faces to the sun. You are a God who hears and answers. Maybe not on my time line or within my plans, but You do answer. Give me patience, Lord. So many before me have blundered badly when their patience failed and they rushed in to "help" Your plans along. I will wait for You, Father, because I trust that You are even now working out the answers. In the name of Jesus, amen.

Day 50
A WAY FOLLOWER

"Blessed be God, who has given peace to his people Israel just as he said he'd do. Not one of all those good and wonderful words that he spoke through Moses has misfired. May God, our very own God, continue to be with us just as he was with our ancestors—may he never give up and walk out on us. May he keep us centered and devoted to him, following the life path he has cleared, watching the signposts, walking at the pace and rhythms he laid down for our ancestors."
1 Kings 8:56–58 msg

My beloved and blessed God, there is no promise You have spoken that You have not also fulfilled. Everything You told Moses would happen happened. You and Your words give me rest from all sides, all quarters, all factions within and without. They are my life and breath. Not only are Your words truth, but they also have the power to calm me, to settle me down and make me content. So continue to be with me, Lord. Don't give up on me, but keep me with You, centered, a follower of Your way. Amen.

Day 51

A GLIMPSE OF A SMILE

A happy heart makes the face cheerful, but heartache crushes
the spirit. The discerning heart seeks knowledge, but the
mouth of a fool feeds on folly. All the days of the oppressed
are wretched, but the cheerful heart has a continual feast.
PROVERBS 15:13–15

I passed my reflection in the mirror, then a storefront window, then the car rearview mirror and noticed my smile. It was missing. In its place was a furrowed brow and focused scowl. How sad. How sad that when I catch a glimpse of my face, it's unsmiling.

God, please forgive me for being so focused on the next task that I forget to carry Your joy on my face. A smile is a free gift—a reminder that *all* of life is a gift. In the morning, Lord, will You please nudge me to first notice Your joy that fills me from the inside? Will You prompt me to dress my face with a smile—a genuine expression that reflects the deep knowledge that the Holy Spirit dwells within me? What do I have to fear? What is more important than this?

God, please continue to use my countenance to display that my soul and smile are from You. In Jesus' name, amen.

Day 52

THE POWER OF PRAISE

"Trust in the Lord your God, and you will be made strong. Trust in the men who speak for Him, and you will do well." . . . [Jehoshaphat] called those who sang to the Lord and those who praised Him in holy clothing. They went out in front of the army and said, "Give thanks to the Lord. For His loving-kindness lasts forever." When they began to sing and praise, the Lord set traps against the men.
2 Chronicles 20:20–22 NLV

It's one thing to read about trusting in You, Lord. It's quite another thing to actually *do* the trusting. That's where I sometimes fall short of how and who You want me to be. Help me work on that, Father. Help me to grow stronger and stronger by trusting You. Help me to be the brave woman You created me to be, one who goes out to meet her enemies while she's singing praises to You. It sounds crazy, but I'm trusting You to make this work and to bring me victory in the process, just as You did for Jehoshaphat and his people who, in the end, "returned to Jerusalem with joy. For the Lord had filled them with joy by saving them" (v. 27). Amen.

Day 53
UNDAUNTED

Therefore we do not lose heart. Though outwardly we are wasting away, yet inwardly we are being renewed day by day. For our light and momentary troubles are achieving for us an eternal glory that far outweighs them all. So we fix our eyes not on what is seen, but on what is unseen, since what is seen is temporary, but what is unseen is eternal.
2 CORINTHIANS 4:16–18

God, our perspective has a way of carving us like a sculptor's chisel. I'm often tempted to fixate on my problems, failures, and hardships. Compared to the comfort and ease of some in this world, the believer's journey can seem rigorous and far too challenging. When I focus on here and now, discouragement edges into my thoughts because I can't see with my eyes the kingdom I'm waiting for. But, Lord, You call this life light and momentary trouble—a passing discomfort that will earn me eternal glory! Instead of straying to the temporary, may my mind be locked on the eternal. Then I will live for You, undaunted by my earthly circumstances, and my soul will be renewed. In Jesus' name, amen.

Day 54
A BETTER PLACE

These mentioned by name were princes in their families; and their fathers' houses increased greatly [so they needed more room]. And they journeyed to the entrance of Gedor. . .to seek pasture for their flocks. And they found rich, good pasture, and the [cleared] land was wide, quiet, and peaceful, because people of Ham had dwelt there of old [and had left it a better place for those who came after them].
1 CHRONICLES 4:38–40 AMPC

We seem, Lord, to be living in an era during which a perfect storm is attacking somewhere every day. Sometimes that storm takes the shape of a tornado, hurricane, earthquake, tsunami, flood, drought, famine, war—you name it. Perhaps if we'd taken better care of the earth, a responsibility You gave us in the beginning, these storms wouldn't be happening. But they are. So, Lord, help me be the kind of woman, the kind of caring being, who leaves this world a better place than she found it. To further that end, Lord, show me how You would have me nurture our earth and, in turn, Your people. In Jesus' name, amen.

Day 55

A HEART OF GRATITUDE

But godliness with contentment is great gain,
for we brought nothing into the world, and we cannot
take anything out of the world. But if we have food
and clothing, with these we will be content.
1 Timothy 6:6–8 esv

God, I confess that today I want ALL THE THINGS. A new house, a new spouse, more space. If I'm being honest, I even want new kids. I want to update my decor and wardrobe and furniture, and even my friends feel old. I'm dissatisfied and embarrassed to admit my feelings. Yet I will, because if I can't be honest with You, who already knows all my thoughts, then who?

Please forgive my selfishness and turn me toward a heart of gratitude. I needn't look far to see how I already have much to be thankful for. God, if I can't be thankful with small things, how am I to be thankful when huge miracles happen? Please tender me to pay attention to the very space I stand, and work outward, noting every person, thing, and circumstance as an absolute gift. Instead of spending energy on what *isn't*, please help me be thankful for all You *have* given. In Jesus' name, amen.

Day 56
HAPPY FOR HOPE

Now that we have been made right with God by putting our trust in Him, we have peace with Him. It is because of what our Lord Jesus Christ did for us. By putting our trust in God, He has given us His loving-favor and has received us. We are happy for the hope we have of sharing the shining-greatness of God. We are glad for our troubles also. We know that troubles help us learn not to give up.
ROMANS 5:1–3 NLV

Oh Lord Jesus, thank You for loving me so much that You died to save my soul. You do all this to make me right with God so that I can have access to Him through prayer and praises. This gives me such peace. It's clear I cannot make it through this life without You by my side, without looking to You for an example of what I am to do and say. Now, as I trust God with all my heart, mind, soul, and strength, I can have joy no matter what my situation. No matter what troubles come against me, I will never give up for I have hope, knowing You will help me through thick and thin, life and death. Amen.

Day 57

THE SPIRIT OF UNDERSTANDING

The Spirit searches all things, even the deep things of God.
For who knows a person's thoughts except their own spirit
within them? In the same way no one knows the thoughts
of God except the Spirit of God. What we have received is
not the spirit of the world, but the Spirit who is from God,
so that we may understand what God has freely given us.
1 CORINTHIANS 2:10–12

God, the world thinks it owns wisdom and understanding, but I know that true understanding of this world and our ultimate destiny comes from You. You authored life, Father. And Your Spirit knows Your thoughts. When I committed my life to You, I received Your Spirit to be my instructor. Show me the deep mysteries of Your ways, Lord. Give me greater understanding of the precious gift You bestowed on me. Because You live in me, I can understand spiritual truths that baffle those who don't know You. The world is confused by You, Lord, because Your ways don't conform to contemporary "wisdom." Thank You for giving me understanding, and help me bring others to You. Amen.

Day 58

MY INNER SELF

*Have mercy on me and be gracious to me, O Lord,
for I am weak (faint and withered away); O Lord, heal
me, for my bones are troubled. My [inner] self [as well as
my body] is also exceedingly disturbed and troubled. But
You, O Lord, how long [until You return and speak peace
to me]? Return [to my relief], O Lord, deliver my life;
save me for the sake of Your steadfast love and mercy.*
PSALM 6:2–4 AMPC

When I am in distress, faint and withering away, come to me, Lord. Heal my body. Give me the physical and mental strength of body and mind that I need to do Your will, to follow Your lead. Calm the storm within my mind, spirit, and heart. Speak words of comfort to my soul. Show me within Your Book the words of peace and love I need to hear, words that will blossom within me, transforming me, helping me to grow more and more into the likeness of Your Son, my master. Deliver me from myself, and pull me up into Your kingdom and grace. In Jesus' name I pray. Amen.

Day 59
A CHANGE IN THE WEATHER

"While the earth remains, seedtime and harvest, cold and heat, summer and winter, day and night, shall not cease."
GENESIS 8:22 ESV

God, the weather is changing. And as it does, would You turn my soul with it? Toward a new way of seeing You? My neighborhood? This community? There's beauty in shifting seasons, for they invite our hearts into a fresh mindset.

Please give me courage to lay down habits and relationships that are heavy and toxic. I'm following You and will continue stepping into this next season with an openness to how You are leading, revealing, and making all things new.

Forgive me for standing stubbornly in security and comfort. I open my hands and heart to You now, even as the temperature and weather change. Please invite me deeper into Your heart, and give me strength to release what I no longer need to grasp tightly so that I may free myself to cling to You. Please use this change in weather to uncover a deeper awareness of You. Amen.

Day 60
GOD'S BLESSINGS

*You shall keep the Feast of Weeks to the Lord your God with
a tribute of a freewill offering from your hand, which you
shall give to the Lord your God, as the Lord your God blesses
you. . . . You shall rejoice in your Feast. . . . Because the Lord
your God will bless you in all your produce and in all the
works of your hands, so that you will be altogether joyful.*
DEUTERONOMY 16:10, 14–15 AMPC

I can't remember the last time I came to You with nothing but
praise and thanks, Lord, for all the ways You've blessed me. Instead, I seem to mostly either unload my troubles or ask You
for things. So today, Lord, I come to You wanting nothing, only
giving You thanks. Thank You for saving me, loving me, protecting me, and watching over me. Thank You for the food, clothing,
and shelter You so sufficiently provide. Thank You for blessings
seen and unseen. And thank You for blessing the work I put my
hands to so that I can be "altogether joyful." What a great God
You are! All praise and glory to You, dear Lord. Amen.

Day 61
PEACE FOREVER

*Of the greatness of his government and peace there
will be no end. He will reign on David's throne and over
his kingdom, establishing and upholding it with justice
and righteousness from that time on and forever.
The zeal of the LORD Almighty will accomplish this.*
ISAIAH 9:7

Father, peace—we all want to live in it, but it seems our lives here are held in the iron grip of calamity. Wars erupt all over the world, and Your followers are increasingly persecuted and criticized. But this shouldn't surprise me. You said to remember that the world hated You before it hated me. And You have promised us a better kingdom, a place where the greatness of Your government and peace will have no end. My mind thrills at the thought of a world swathed in peace. No fighting. No killing. No arguing. No jealousy and gossip and petty backbiting. Harmony will reign supreme. Lord, I long to dwell in this place with You. In Jesus' name, amen.

Day 62

BOOMERANG

Go your way; behold, I send you out like lambs into the midst of wolves. . . . Whatever house you enter, first say, Peace be to this household! [Freedom from all the distresses that result from sin be with this family]. And if anyone [worthy] of peace and blessedness is there, the peace and blessedness you wish shall come upon him; but if not, it shall come back to you.
LUKE 10:3, 5–6 AMPC

What a wonderful way to spread Your peace, Lord, by taking it on the road. You have a direction for me to take. A path to follow. My job and joy are to trust and follow Your leading. So show me, Lord, where You would have me go, which household You would have me reach out to. Then give me courage to enter into the unknown there and to bless that household with Your peace. . . . Yet if Your peace and blessing are neither wanted nor warranted by that household, I thank You for setting things up so that the peace and blessedness I wish upon others will come back upon me. That's a boomerang result I'll never dodge. Amen!

Day 63
ABIDING

"Abide in me, and I in you. As the branch cannot bear fruit by itself, unless it abides in the vine, neither can you, unless you abide in me. I am the vine; you are the branches. Whoever abides in me and I in him, he it is that bears much fruit."
JOHN 15:4–5 ESV

Jesus, I like the idea of abiding, but doing it is another matter altogether. Abiding means to endure, to stay the course and cling to You for the long haul. Lord, I confess, I want the quick answers, the blessings to abound. I want the flowers before I've done the long work of being tucked into the soil and taking long days, darkness, and time to bloom.

What is it about abiding that I'm fighting? What part is hard? Jesus, as I notice this push against staying in You, I sense that the waiting and depending cause anxiety. How long do I need to abide? When will the fruit come?

Forgive me for focusing on the fruit instead of melting into Your branches. How I long to rest in Your love and let Your work be done in Your time, so that You are the one who is glorified. Amen.

Day 64
SINGING AND DANCING

David went everywhere that Saul sent him, and did well. Saul had him lead the men of war. And it was pleasing to all the people and to Saul's servants. When David returned from killing the Philistine, the women came out of all the cities of Israel, singing and dancing, to meet King Saul, playing songs of joy on timbrels. The women sang as they played, and said, "Saul has killed his thousands, and David his ten thousands."
1 SAMUEL 18:5–7 NLV

It's so easy to cheer for and celebrate people who play sports or act on stage and screen. But when it comes to celebrating You, Lord, I seem to hesitate, wondering what people will think of me. Help me to change that up, dear God. I want to be like the women who sang and danced with abandon back in David's day. Doing so not only pleases You but fills me with such joy, lifting me higher in mind, spirit, and body. It's a win-win for both of us, Lord. So I come to You with abandon today, dancing as I sing my song of praise just for You! Amen.

Day 65

CONFIDENT HOPE

Faith shows the reality of what we hope for; it is the evidence of things we cannot see. Through their faith, the people in days of old earned a good reputation.
HEBREWS 11:1–2 NLT

Heavenly Father, I praise Your name that there's no such thing as blind faith in You. You haven't left me with no assurance that what You've promised will come true. Instead, You've shown me Your stellar record of thousands of years of promise keeping in the Bible. How could I not trust that kind of integrity? You do and have always done what You say You will do. I have confidence that what I hope for is real. Eternity with You is real. You are really there for me, God. You've given me evidence of the things I can't see through my faith in You. My doubts have fled in the face of overwhelming evidence that You exist. In Jesus' holy name, amen.

Day 66
EVEN THEN

The Lord is my Light and my Salvation—whom shall I fear or dread? The Lord is the Refuge and Stronghold of my life—of whom shall I be afraid? . . . Though a host encamp against me, my heart shall not fear; though war arise against me, [even then] in this will I be confident. One thing have I asked of the Lord, that will I seek, inquire for, and [insistently] require: that I may dwell. . .[in His presence] all the days of my life.
PSALM 27:1, 3-4 AMPC

You, Lord, are the one who divided the Red Sea, stopped the sun, and sent chariots of fire to protect Your prophet. Throughout the ages, You've continuously proven Yourself to be the God of all gods! Thus, with You on my side, I need have no fear. In fact, I am calm. For there's no one who can outdo You, God Almighty. Even if I'm caught in a war, *even then* I'll be at peace within because You're here to help me, to pull me into Your safety net. Continue to be with me, Lord, loving me, holding me, calming me all the days of my life, to the end. Even then. Amen.

Day 67
EAGER TO EXPERIENCE

"For the ear tests words as the palate tastes food."
JOB 34:3 ESV

God, I wake eager to experience You in the tiny details of today. Before I get out of bed, would You please clear my mind of clutter and distractions so that I can approach the day open and ready to listen. As I go about work, cleaning, everyday tasks, would You help me notice how Your Spirit meets me in my senses?

Where am I hearing You? What are You saying? What smells evoke memories of when I'm most alive? What tangible things do I touch that turn a grateful heart to You? What am I reading, and is it truth-honoring? Are the foods I eat out of coping or nourishment?

Please help me notice the personal ways You woo me and meet me right where I am: shopping at the grocery store, talking with a coworker, and preparing dinner. I often neglect to say yes to Your all-sensory invitations knocking at every turn. Still my heart to notice, and may I answer with anticipation and a gladness of spirit. In Jesus' name, amen.

Day 68

TURNED HEARTS

They finished their building by decree of the God of Israel and by decree of Cyrus and Darius and Artaxerxes king of Persia. . . . And the people of Israel. . .celebrated the dedication of this house of God with joy. . . . For the LORD had made them joyful and had turned the heart of the king of Assyria to them, so that he aided them in the work of the house of God.
EZRA 6:14, 16, 22 ESV

Only You, Lord, have the power to turn the hearts of rulers, whether they be queens, presidents, tyrants, or dictators, so that Your work can be accomplished through them and us. This gives me hope that You can turn even the most godless person to help Your people do what You have called them to do, no matter how great the task. And that hope in You and Your power working to change people, against all odds and appearances to the contrary, gives me great joy. For with You, nothing is impossible. In Your power, I not only rest but go forward with confidence, hope, and joy. In Jesus' name, amen.

Day 69
PRAISE HIM

As for me, I will always have hope; I will praise you more and more. My mouth will tell of your righteous deeds, of your saving acts all day long— though I know not how to relate them all.
PSALM 71:14–15

Lord, praising You is the best cure for depression and despair. I often become enmeshed in my own problems and all that is wrong in the world and forget how great You are. But today I choose praise over melancholy. As the psalmist wrote, "I will always have hope." God, I am saved. I am redeemed. I am chosen. I am forgiven. You love me so much that You gave Your life in ransom for mine and are even now preparing a beautiful home for me in eternity. I don't deserve any of this! In fact, what I deserve is punishment, but You've given me grace instead. And on top of Your mercy You've poured good gifts upon me. Praise You, Jesus. Amen.

Day 70
A PLAIN AND EVEN PATH

*In the day of trouble He will hide me in His shelter;
in the secret place of His tent will He hide me; He will
set me high upon a rock. . . . Although my father and
my mother have forsaken me, yet the Lord will take
me up [adopt me as His child]. Teach me Your way,
O Lord, and lead me in a plain and even path.*
PSALM 27:5, 10–11 AMPC

When trouble comes, hide me, Lord. Shelter me in Your secret place, high up, way beyond the reach of those who want to harm me. And in that place, Lord, give me the wisdom I need to regain my footing. Remind me that, although members of my family, friends, and others I have known may abandon me, *You* will never do so. For You are my Abba. You've adopted me into Your family. What comfort, what peace I find in knowing that I will never be alone, that I will always have You. So, Lord, walk me down that plain and even path I share with You. Amen.

Day 71
SELF—CONTROL

For the Spirit God gave us does not make us timid,
but gives us power, love and self-discipline.
2 Timothy 1:7

God, I'm sorry. I acknowledge that I need self-control. I'm prone to react and impatiently tap my foot and yell when I'm not getting my way. I'm like a toddler having an adult temper tantrum. I'm embarrassed to see this ugliness surface, but it's true.

Please forgive me for being quick to blame or pick up the phone to complain to a friend. Please draw me to vent to You first, bringing my frustrations to safely process in Your presence. Thank You for accepting all of me—even the parts that need pruning of selfishness.

Where do I need to control my tongue? My emotions? My reactions? Speak to me about how I can practice self-control. Thank You for the grace You pour out as I yearn to be molded into Your likeness. In Jesus' name, amen.

Day 72
MORNING MOMENTS

*In the morning You hear my voice, O Lord; in the morning
I prepare [a prayer, a sacrifice] for You and watch and
wait [for You to speak to my heart]. . . . Let all those
who take refuge and put their trust in You rejoice;
let them ever sing and shout for joy, because You make a
covering over them and defend them; let those also who
love Your name be joyful in You and be in high spirits.*
PSALM 5:3, 11 AMPC

In these early morning moments, Lord, I come to You. Hear my voice. I'm giving You my all—my heart, soul, body, and mind. I await Your presence. Come to me, Lord. Speak gently, softly, to my heart. Tell me the words You want me to hear as I take refuge in You, laying down all my burdens and taking up Your strength, courage, and love. Fill me with Your Spirit. Shield me from any dangers that may come. Help me stay attuned to You all through this day. Lord, I love You ever so much, to the moon and back and more. For it is with and in You that I find my true joy every moment of the day. Amen.

Day 73
MY SALVATION

The Lord is good to those whose hope is in him,
to the one who seeks him; it is good to wait
quietly for the salvation of the Lord.
LAMENTATIONS 3:25–26

Lord, Your goodness flows to those who depend on You and search for You. In my stubbornness, I try to do things my own way and believe I can be self-reliant. I quote Your Word as "I can do all things" and too often conveniently forget the "through Christ who strengthens me" part. I think that I should be my own answer and create all my own solutions. And when the plates I'm spinning shatter at my feet, I remember to seek You. Lord, You are my answer and the solution to every problem. Help me to seek You more and trust that You have everything in hand. Any control I think I have is an illusion anyway. So I wait for You. In Jesus' name, amen.

Day 74
STANDING WORD

"I tell from the beginning what will happen in the end. And from times long ago I tell of things which have not been done, saying, 'My Word will stand. And I will do all that pleases Me.' I call a strong and hungry bird from the east, the man from a far country who will do what I have planned. I have spoken, and I will make it happen. I have planned it, and I will do it."
ISAIAH 46:10–11 NLV

Lord, it's amazing how well Your Bible books fit together. How the Old Testament supports the New. How the psalms soothe minds, bodies, souls, and spirits unlike any other book. How the Gospels tell Your story with four different audiences in mind. How the letters to the New Testament churches tell us how to live, and how Jesus' revelation tells us what to expect when He returns. Lord, Your Word not only stands but transforms—people as well as circumstances. What You have said, You *will* make happen. What You have planned, You *will* do. Help me to rest in the peace of that promise, Lord. Speak to me; tell me what part You would have me play in Your plan. In Jesus' name, amen.

Day 75

THE HEALING SIDE OF SILENCE

*It is good that one should wait quietly
for the salvation of the Lord.*
LAMENTATIONS 3:26 ESV

In my younger years, silence scared me. Words affirmed and told me I was on the right track. In maturity, God, please invite me to see silence as a chance to hear from You. I long to know what Your voice sounds like, and I can't if I'm constantly distracted with noise, media, or voices filling the room and my thoughts.

Your silence is where I can learn to discern my own thoughts and Yours. What do You wish to say today? Perhaps I need to carve out quiet time to simply be with You. To sit in Your love and feel it down to my bones. To saturate myself in the psalms and accept this space of silence as sacred ground. However You wish to meet me, I am here, open and listening. God, forgive me for being afraid of what silence brings. Please show me the healing side of silence now. In Jesus' name, amen.

Day 76
A GLAD HEART

*A glad heart makes a cheerful countenance, but by
sorrow of heart the spirit is broken. . . . All the days of
the desponding and afflicted are made evil [by anxious
thoughts and forebodings], but he who has a glad heart
has a continual feast [regardless of circumstances].
Better is little with the reverent, worshipful fear of the
Lord than great and rich treasure and trouble with it.*
PROVERBS 15:13, 15–16 AMPC

Abba, some days I find myself brought so low by what's happening in the world. And sometimes my chin is on the floor because of what's happening in my home, my family, or my work. More often than not, my mind is filled with anxious thoughts and forebodings. But I don't want to live that way. I want to have a glad heart, no matter what's happening. So I need Your help to focus on the good things, the things above, not the things of this earth. Help me, Lord, not to worry about anything—money, relationships, wars, or other troubles—but to keep my chin up by keeping my eyes and focus on You alone. In Jesus' name, amen.

Day 77
HE IS LIGHT

This is the message we have heard from him and declare to you: God is light; in him there is no darkness at all. If we claim to have fellowship with him and yet walk in the darkness, we lie and do not live out the truth. But if we walk in the light, as he is in the light, we have fellowship with one another, and the blood of Jesus, his Son, purifies us from all sin.
1 John 1:5–7

Heavenly Father, sometimes I forget who You are and apply human standards to Your character. But Your Word promises that You are light and only light. Nothing dark can coexist with You. This news is so wonderful because it means that I can trust You fully. You have no selfish or evil ulterior motives for anything that You do. Everything You say is truth. I can have a relationship with You, my friend, the one who has robed me in borrowed righteousness and forgiven every wrong deed I've ever committed. Strengthen me to walk in Your light. My sinful nature is tempted by the darkness, but I want to keep to the light, Father! In Jesus' name, amen.

Day 78
QUIETING DOWN

Open up before GOD, keep nothing back; he'll do whatever needs to be done: He'll validate your life in the clear light of day and stamp you with approval at high noon. Quiet down before GOD, be prayerful before him. Don't bother with those who climb the ladder, who elbow their way to the top. Bridle your anger, trash your wrath, cool your pipes—it only makes things worse. Before long the crooks will be bankrupt; GOD-investors will soon own the store.
PSALM 37:5–9 MSG

I can't take it, Lord. Nor do I understand it. Why do those who are evil have the best lives? They seem to have everything they could ever want or need, while so many believers, like me, struggle every day just to survive. Yet You tell me not to worry about those who step on other people to get ahead in this world. So. . .I won't. Instead of ranting at the prosperity of evildoers, I'm going to quiet down before You, settle into Your peace. Because I know that, in the end, all those who follow You alone will have the true reward: a place in eternity with You. In Jesus' name I pray. Amen!

Day 79
THE GREAT HEALER

The Lord appeared to us in the past, saying:
"I have loved you with an everlasting love;
I have drawn you with unfailing kindness."
JEREMIAH 31:3

God, there are pains that I thought had healed, and out of nowhere, *pop!* They surface! I'm left wondering what happened and what I could have done differently.

I recognize healing is a continual process. Would You search my heart and offer insight into where I need to accept and confess responsibility? Where do I need to forgive? How do I need to grow? And the ache of pain that still exists—Lord, would You please heal those tender places? Would You bring people to speak love and grace into the parts that are deeply wounded? Would You speak truth and help me lay down the lies I'm falsely believing or the extra weight I no longer need to carry?

You are the Great Healer, and my soul aches for Your restoration. I ask You to meet me in this continual healing journey. May I lean on You when the pain is too great and rest in Your unconditional arms of love. In Jesus' name, amen.

Day 80

IN THE ARMS OF THE BELOVED SHEPHERD

Like an apple tree among the trees of the wood, so is my beloved [shepherd] among the sons [cried the girl]! Under his shadow I delighted to sit, and his fruit was sweet to my taste. . . . His banner over me was love [for love waved as a protecting and comforting banner over my head when I was near him]. . . . [I can feel] his left hand under my head and his right hand embraces me!
SONG OF SOLOMON 2:3–4, 6 AMPC

Beloved Shepherd, I find more delight, more joy in Your presence than anywhere else. For You have told me of Your deep love, which will never die but will continue to protect and comfort me whenever You are near. So I come to You in this tender and precious moment. I can feel Your left hand under my head and Your right hand pulling me close into Your loving embrace. As my head rests against Your breast, I rise and fall with each of Your breaths. Hold me close, Lord. Keep me safe as I linger here in Your presence, safe in body, sound in mind, and happy in heart. Amen.

Day 81
LIVING WATER

*Jesus answered, "Everyone who drinks this water will be
thirsty again, but whoever drinks the water I give them
will never thirst. Indeed, the water I give them will become
in them a spring of water welling up to eternal life."*
JOHN 4:13–14

Jesus, You gave this woman at the well such hope. She was
searching for fulfillment and dying of thirst for something
greater, much like all of us today. To never thirst again for ac-
ceptance. To never thirst again for forgiveness. To never thirst
again for love. To have a life of eternity. You have quenched
these needs and so many others, Jesus. You are the living water.
I can drink of Your message and go away satisfied. I will never
thirst for anything else now that I have known You. I can no longer seek meaning in houses or money or any of the empty idols
I have chased. Knowing You has unveiled the true reality of my
existence. In Jesus' name, amen.

Day 82
FREEING UP

Take heed to yourselves and be on your guard, lest your hearts be overburdened and depressed (weighed down) with. . .worldly worries and cares pertaining to [the business of] this life. . . . Keep awake then and watch at all times [be discreet, attentive, and ready], praying that you may have the full strength and ability and be accounted worthy to escape all these things [taken together] that will take place, and to stand in the presence of the Son of Man.
LUKE 21:34, 36 AMPC

I need Your help, Lord. I'm getting so weighed down by the news of what's happening in the town and country I live in and beyond. It's so depressing. Yet I'm pretty sure I wasn't made to take on all the troubles of this world. My frame wasn't built to bear the weight of that load. So help me, Lord, to turn my eyes from troubles and focus on You. Give me the words to pray when I hear bad news from any quarter—local or foreign. Tell me how to help humans, animals, and nature. Help me stay awake and aware of You so that I will have the strength to do Your will. In Jesus' name, amen.

Day 83

A SPARK OF FUN AND LAUGHTER

*So, whether you eat or drink, or whatever
you do, do all to the glory of God.*
1 CORINTHIANS 10:31 ESV

God, I could use some fun in my life. Some laughter and joy and a spark of hope. What is clouding the joy and stealing the celebration of today? Help me stay here long enough to ponder the deeper places of my heart and pull out the melancholy parts.

You don't ask me to get rid of my authentic emotions or stitch on a fake smile. You desire true life to bubble out of me, and I desperately want that. Please nudge me toward what will bring a sense of fun today. A nature walk? Baking? Going out with a friend? Tackling a creative project?

You know me best. I bring my bad attitude to You now and thank You for welcoming all of me. Invite me to note the spark of fun You long to join me in, and give me tenacity to embrace it with passion and curiosity. You are a Father who is fun and loves to delight in Your daughter. Amen.

Day 84
RISING UP TO THE LOVE

Arise, my love, my fair one, and come away. [So I went with him, and when we were climbing the rocky steps up the hillside, my beloved shepherd said to me] O my dove, [while you are here]. . .in the sheltered and secret place of the cliff, let me see your face, let me hear your voice; for your voice is sweet, and your face is lovely. [My heart was touched and I fervently sang to him my desire].
SONG OF SOLOMON 2:13–15 AMPC

It fills me with joy, Lord, that You call me "my love." That You want me to come away with You to that secret place where we meet, just You and me alone. That You want to see my face and hear my voice. That You think I'm lovely. Thank You, my beloved, for calling me to rise up to You and tell You about my desires and all the things that are on my heart. There is nothing and no one like You, Lord. To You alone I bear all my secrets, all my longings, knowing that You will not laugh at them but will treasure them. Dear heart, I love You. Amen.

Day 85
SEEK AND FIND

"Ask and it will be given to you; seek and you will find;
knock and the door will be opened to you. For everyone
who asks receives; the one who seeks finds; and to
the one who knocks, the door will be opened."
MATTHEW 7:7–8

Lord, You don't make Yourself elusive to us. You don't hide and evade our searching hearts. Instead, You promise that if we seek we will find. You will open the door and introduce Yourself to any stranger who knocks. God, how astonishing to realize that a small, seemingly insignificant speck of Your creation like me can know and have a relationship with the eternal God of the universe. I'm humbled that You would answer my probing knocks and invite me in to know You better. You want me to know You deeply and fully and to experience the fathomless depth of Your pure love for me. You desire a genuine relationship. Thank You, God, for the honor of calling You friend. In Jesus' name, amen.

Day 86

A HAPPY WOMAN OF PEACE

The steps of a [good] man are directed and established by the Lord when He delights in his way [and He busies Himself with his every step]. Though he falls, he shall not be utterly cast down, for the Lord grasps his hand in support and upholds him. . . . Mark the blameless man and behold the upright, for there is a happy end for the man of peace.
PSALM 37:23–24, 37 AMPC

What a relief, Lord! The idea that You direct my steps makes me feel so content. Because if You're delighting in my way and walking with me, I know I can have peace about today and tomorrow. For You are with me with each step I take. And even if I trip up or fall, You'll pull me back onto my feet! You, Lord, are my main support. You are what motivates me, drives me, comforts me, and secures me. Thank You, Lord, for always being here for me, for making me a happy woman of peace in You. Amen.

Day 87

A TENDER SPIRIT

"Flesh gives birth to flesh, but the Spirit gives birth to spirit. You should not be surprised at my saying, 'You must be born again.' The wind blows wherever it pleases. You hear its sound, but you cannot tell where it comes from or where it is going. So it is with everyone born of the Spirit."

JOHN 3:6–8

Lord, I'm used to how I do things. How I think. How I feel. So much *I, I, I.* I confess my comfortable ways and offer myself to You now. Please forgive me for being too rigid at times, too stubborn.

How can I tender my spirit? My will? My habits? My thoughts? What coping mechanisms need to be shaved off for surrender to be put in their place? Where are You inviting me to be malleable to Your will?

I offer my stubbornness and ask You to make me tender, sensitive to Your Spirit, willing to change my ways and listen more and speak less. Where do I need to soften? Let go? Shift directions? Please offer Your Spirit-breathed discernment and strength to soften the edges of my heart that have become hard. Mold me to be more like You, Jesus. Amen.

Day 88
A HEART AWAKE

I went to sleep, but my heart stayed awake. [I dreamed that I heard] the voice of my beloved as he knocked [at the door of my mother's cottage]. Open to me, my sister, my love, my dove, my spotless one [he said]. . . . [But weary from a day in the vineyards, I had already sought my rest] I had put off my garment—how could I [again] put it on? I had washed my feet—how could I [again] soil them?
SONG OF SOLOMON 5:2–3 AMPC

Lord, in Your presence I experience such unfathomable joy. Yet at times I am so worn out from earthly cares that I do not open my door to You. In those moments, I miss out on Your peace, calm, wisdom, power, strength, and gentle touch. Even in the night hours, asleep or awake, I want to be available to You—to Your voice, Your whisper, Your knock on my door. Help me keep attuned to Your quest for me. May my spirit be so linked to Yours that I don't know where I stop and You begin. I pray this in Jesus' precious name, amen.

Day 89

THE PROMISE OF PARADISE

*One of the criminals who hung there hurled insults
at him. . . . But the other criminal rebuked him.
"Don't you fear God," he said, "since you are under
the same sentence? We are punished justly, for we are
getting what our deeds deserve. But this man has done
nothing wrong." Then he said, "Jesus, remember me when
you come into your kingdom." Jesus answered him,
"Truly I tell you, today you will be with me in paradise."*
LUKE 23:39–43

Father, beside Your innocent Son hung two criminals on crosses just like His. Two men who had lived sinful, evil lives. One of them entered paradise with You and one did not. By his own admission, they deserved their punishment. But the only thing that mattered at the gates of paradise was not an impressive résumé of goodness but rather his belief in You as the Lamb who takes away the sins of the world. Thank You, Jesus, that You took God's wrath and my punishment upon Yourself. Thank You that I don't have to be good enough, because I can't be. I've earned my punishment just like those two men who died with You, but You gave me life instead of death, paradise instead of punishment. Amen.

Day 90
GETTING A GRIP

*There's one other thing I remember, and remembering,
I keep a grip on hope: GOD's loyal love couldn't have run
out, his merciful love couldn't have dried up. They're
created new every morning. How great your faithfulness!
I'm sticking with GOD (I say it over and over). He's all
I've got left. GOD proves to be good to the man who
passionately waits, to the woman who diligently seeks.*
LAMENTATIONS 3:21–25 MSG

Some days, Lord, it seems relatively easy to lose hope. The problems to be tackled seem to be growing by the minute. It's enough to make even the strongest of believers despair! But I'm leaning into You, Lord. I'm remembering how every morning with You is a new beginning. Because You have unlimited mercy and love, You create them new every morning! That's how faithful You are to me even when I might hesitate to be faithful to You! Forgive me, Lord, for my missteps. For You are my all in all, my greatest hope, my everlasting love. I will continue to seek You and adore You always, for in You I find my peace. Amen.

Day 91

COFFEE TIME

*The steadfast love of the L*ORD *never ceases;*
his mercies never come to an end; they are new
every morning; great is your faithfulness.
LAMENTATIONS 3:22–23 ESV

Today is a new day, and as I pour myself a cup of coffee, may I quiet myself before You, Lord. Help me offer You the first morning moments and find truth in Your Word.

What verses are You drawing me to? What are You saying today? What do I need to put aside so I can come, expectant and open, before You? What are the longings and desires of my heart? How are You inviting me to pray?

Please quiet my soul and use this coffee time to create a morning rhythm where I bring myself to You and allow You to fill me before I work, parent, create, and beyond.

As I pour my coffee, I imagine You pouring my being to the fullness of Your grace, Your love, Your power. As I drink my coffee, may I take quiet moments to prepare my heart to move about my day staying filled by You and refilling when I find my strength low and in need of Your renewed presence. Amen.

Day 92
JOYFULLY RADIANT

[She proudly said] I am my beloved's, and his desire is toward me! . . . Many waters cannot quench love, neither can floods drown it. . . . [Joyfully the radiant bride turned to him, the one altogether lovely, the chief among ten thousand to her soul, and with unconcealed eagerness to begin her life of sweet companionship with him, she answered] Make haste, my beloved, and come quickly, like a gazelle or a young hart [and take me to our waiting home].
SONG OF SOLOMON 7:10; 8:7, 14 AMPC

The fact that You desire me, Lord, fills me with such delight. I rejoice that I am Yours and You are mine and that the love we have for each other can never disappear. I am so eager to turn to You, to begin our life together each morning. Take me to that rock that is higher than I, that secret place where it is only You and me, together forever. That is my true home, my true abode where nothing untoward can touch me and where You cover me with Your love. You dry my tears and simply hold me, telling me all is well and will be well. You are my heaven on earth. Amen.

Day 93
SHOUTS OF JOY

*"He will yet fill your mouth with laughter
and your lips with shouts of joy."*
JOB 8:21

Loving Father in heaven, thank You for blessing me with the gifts of laughter and hope. You haven't called me to an existence of joyless solemnity, but instead You came to give life—a full and everlasting life of hope in You. Sometimes I allow my difficulties and pain to rob me of the hope that lives within me. But no longer! I rejoice in You always because the goodness You have waiting for me in heaven is unimaginable to my fragile human mind. You have given me a new spiritual life right now that spills over to a dark world filled with others searching for peace and hope found only in You. In the name of Jesus, amen.

Day 94
ENTER THE SILENCE

*It's a good thing to quietly hope, quietly hope for help from
God. It's a good thing when you're young to stick it out
through the hard times. When life is heavy and hard to take,
go off by yourself. Enter the silence. Bow in prayer. Don't
ask questions: Wait for hope to appear. Don't run from
trouble. Take it full-face. The "worst" is never the worst.*
LAMENTATIONS 3:26–30 MSG

It's been a long few days, Lord. And I need some time away with
You. Some time to sit quietly and tap into Your power and grace,
to reacquaint myself with Your Word and the hope I find there.
I need to step back, step away from the daily grind, even if only
for a moment. Perhaps only for this very moment. Right here,
right now, Lord, I come to You. I enter the silence, and I bow in
prayer. Here I await Your blessing of hope, confidence, courage,
and trust. In Jesus' name, I wait and pray. Amen.

Day 95
HONEST BREATHS

"This is what the Sovereign Lord says to these bones:
I will make breath enter you, and you will come to life."
Ezekiel 37:5

Lord, please give me Your breath today. I'm exhaling heavy breaths of worry, anxiety, pride, and judgment. I'm breathing out jealousy, comparison, doubt, fear, and shame. I give all these honest breaths to You.

Help me, Lord, to breathe in Your truths: Your patience, love, peace, grace, beauty, and awareness. Help me breathe in forgiveness of self and others. Help me breathe in sensitivity to Your voice, Your movements, Your invitations. Help me breathe in purity of thoughts, words, and actions. Help me breathe in compassion, truth, mercy, and steadfastness.

I breathe out anything that's not of You and breathe in all that is of You—of light, of purity, of beauty. Forgive me for taking breaths for granted. Spirit of the living God, breathe afresh on me now. In Jesus' name, amen.

Day 96

BEYOND UNDERSTANDING

*Be full of joy always because you belong to the Lord.
Again I say, be full of joy! Let all people see how
gentle you are. . . . Do not worry. Learn to pray about
everything. Give thanks to God as you ask Him for
what you need. The peace of God is much greater
than the human mind can understand. This peace will
keep your hearts and minds through Christ Jesus.*
PHILIPPIANS 4:4–7 NLV

Joy, at times, seems elusive, Lord. But that's only because I for-get to call on You, my champion, my master, my Creator, the All-Powerful One who makes the seemingly impossible possi-ble! Instead of running to You, I let my worries begin a running dialogue in my head. Soon they spin out of control and build up to a sort of mild panic. Help me, Lord, to learn to pray about anything and everything—and to thank You in the process. Your Word says that if I do, Your peace beyond understanding will surround me and guard me. So here I am, Lord, telling You all, thanking You for all. . . . Ah, now it's time to rejoice! Amen.

Day 97
MADE NEW

*Therefore, if anyone is in Christ, the new creation has come:
The old has gone, the new is here! All this is from God, who
reconciled us to himself through Christ and gave us the
ministry of reconciliation: that God was reconciling the world
to himself in Christ, not counting people's sins against them.
And he has committed to us the message of reconciliation.*
2 CORINTHIANS 5:17–19

God, I'm broken. I live in a broken world. I'm enmeshed in an existence filled with war and hatred, messed-up families, selfishness, and abuse. I've tried to fix the brokenness in my life. I've run after success and relationships, but I can't mend what's wrong by using the things of this world. I can't mend the sin in my life. But You can, Jesus. God, all I have to do is surrender to You and repent. You came and died so that I could be regenerated into something new in Christ. You have a plan of redemption for this world, Father. I'm not broken anymore! I have been remade in Jesus. Reconciled to God. I am new! In Jesus' name, amen.

Day 98
BLAST FROM THE PAST

*One thing I do: Forgetting what is behind and reaching
forward to what is ahead, I pursue as my goal the
prize promised by God's heavenly call in Christ Jesus.
Therefore, all who are mature should think this way.
And if you think differently about anything, God
will reveal this also to you. In any case, we should
live up to whatever truth we have attained.*
PHILIPPIANS 3:13–16 HCSB

Too often, Lord, my past encroaches upon then disrupts my present. The mistakes I had once made, the consequences that followed keep reverberating in my head. That sometimes makes it difficult for me to keep my focus on You, the present, and what You'd have me do in the moments that make up my day. So help me, Lord, to find my peace by forgetting what has happened before, what cannot be undone, and then help me reach forward to what lies ahead of me as I follow after You. Show me, Lord. Reveal Yourself and Your plan to me. Point out to me the way You'd have me go as I blast away from the past. Amen.

Day 99
HUNGER FOR TRUTH

Do your best to present yourself to God as one
approved, a worker who does not need to be ashamed
and who correctly handles the word of truth.
2 Timothy 2:15

I'm becoming aware of my hunger for truth. For real, black-and-white, scriptural, I-feel-lighter-inside truth. Truth that comes only from You. Authentic. Pure.

I apologize, Lord, for my ease to accept as truth much of what I hear or read. I even make assumptions about my worth based on others' response to me instead of going to You first.

Turn my heart now and stir me toward truth. Where do I need to turn off untruthful voices and noise and turn on Your truth filter? Where in Your Word are You beckoning me to read and stay? What truth are You filling my mind, eyes, and heart with? What untruths have I been believing? Where are You longing to replace these lies with the reality of Your unconditional love? Lead me to Your truth, which is everlasting and freeing, indeed. In Jesus' name, amen.

Day 100
HUMBLY BLESSED

*He opened His mouth and taught them, saying: Blessed
(happy, to be envied, and spiritually prosperous—with
life-joy and satisfaction in God's favor and salvation,
regardless of their outward conditions) are the poor in
spirit (the humble, who rate themselves insignificant),
for theirs is the kingdom of heaven! . . . He poured water
into the washbasin and began to wash the disciples'
feet and to wipe them with the [servant's] towel.*
MATTHEW 5:2–3; JOHN 13:5 AMPC

Jesus, I can't imagine being one of the disciples whose feet You washed. It seems incomprehensible that You, the Son of God, would kneel before one of Your brothers or sisters and wash his or her dirty, stinky feet. Yet that's just what You did—providing the example I am to follow as Your disciple. Help me, Lord, to have a servant's heart and to humble myself, kneeling before someone who needs my help, no matter who or what that person is. For I want to share in Your joy, to be blessed in and with You, and to gain the kingdom of heaven! In Your name, amen.

Day 101
LOVED

There is no fear in love. But perfect love drives out fear, because fear has to do with punishment. The one who fears is not made perfect in love. We love because he first loved us.
1 JOHN 4:18–19

Father, You loved me first. I can't work my way into Your affections. And I don't have to! You have always loved me. You loved me so fully that Your Son took the punishment that was meant for me. Your perfect love drives away all my fears. You loved me even though I am a sinner. I will never be perfect on this earth. But I am forgiven. When You look at me, You no longer see the ragged, dirty shreds of sin I was garbed in. Now You see the pristine, shining righteousness of Your Son. Father, fill me with Your love and allow it to overflow the borders of my life onto everyone I meet. In the name of Jesus, amen.

Day 102

STANDING BY

The Lord stood by me and strengthened me, so that through me the [Gospel] message might be fully proclaimed and all the Gentiles might hear it. So I was delivered out of the jaws of the lion. [And indeed] the Lord will certainly deliver and draw me to Himself from every assault of evil. He will preserve and bring me safe unto His heavenly kingdom. To Him be the glory forever and ever. Amen (so be it).
2 Timothy 4:17–18 ampc

People come and go throughout my life, but You, Lord, are always here with me. You're the one standing by me, giving me the courage to do what You've called me to do. You give me the confidence to stand my ground, to face whatever comes against me. Because You've delivered me in the past, so I know You'll do it in the present and future. Best of all, Your presence of light and love reminds me that even if things don't go the way I think they should, all is and will be well because You have the best plan for me. In all this I find an undefinable and undeniable peace. Amen.

Day 103

ALL THE ANSWERS

Humble yourselves before the Lord, and he will exalt you.
JAMES 4:10 ESV

God, I want control. I want to know how life will unfold. I want to have answers for all my questions. How long do I have to wait? What is Your plan? Why am I sitting in the quiet? Where is Your Spirit beckoning?

Do You hear all my questions and the anxiety underneath? Forgive me, God, for worrying—for clinging to answers more than Your presence. Draw me to curl up with You now. To simply be with You and enjoy Your presence, not for the answers I get but for the intimacy that comes from sitting with You. Where I'm anxious for answers, please whisper that You are the answer—that You know my needs and will take care of me.

I surrender my control. I surrender my angst. I surrender my worry and frantic anxiety. I surrender my need to rush to the next answer before waiting for You to respond. I surrender my security in needing to have a plan. I surrender to You. Amen.

Day 104
WORDS OF JOY

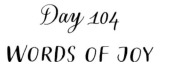

O Lord, You know and understand; [earnestly] remember me and visit me and avenge me on my persecutors. Take me not away [from joy or from life itself] in Your long-suffering [to my enemies]; know that for Your sake I suffer and bear reproach. Your words were found, and I ate them; and Your words were to me a joy and the rejoicing of my heart, for I am called by Your name, O Lord God of hosts.
JEREMIAH 15:15–16 AMPC

God, I am so glad You can see what I'm going through, all the things I'm up against. You know how my troubles are zapping my joy. But then I reach for Your Word. I open Your Book and discover You. Letter by letter, word by word, sentence by sentence, I absorb all You have to say to me—how You love and work with me, how You want all that is good to come to me. You even have a plan for me. And it is here, within Your Word and presence, that I find the joy I need to live this life. Thank You for allowing me to hear Your voice and find my way home to You. Amen.

Day 105
HE IS GOD

He says, "Be still, and know that I am God; I will be exalted among the nations, I will be exalted in the earth." The LORD Almighty is with us; the God of Jacob is our fortress.
PSALM 46:10–11

Lord, You are God and I am not. That realization brings me peace and hope and security. I don't have to attempt to control the universe. I can simply be still and recognize Your ultimate power and authority. I trust You, loving Father, to attend to the details of my life. I can't pretend to understand the intricacies of Your plans. Indeed, who am I to question them? But I can rest in my knowledge of Your good character. The weight of chasing my destiny and forging my path has been lifted since I put my trust in You. You are all-powerful and limitless in all Your ways. You are my God. In Jesus' name, amen.

Day 106
PERSONAL KNOWLEDGE

Because he has set his love upon Me, therefore will I deliver him; I will set him on high, because he knows and understands My name [has a personal knowledge of My mercy, love, and kindness—trusts and relies on Me, knowing I will never forsake him, no, never]. He shall call upon Me, and I will answer him; I will be with him in trouble, I will deliver him.
PSALM 91:14–15 AMPC

The more I learn about You, Lord, the more I love You. The more I understand what You have done for me, the more I trust You. There are, of course, some things I may never know, but I'm okay with that because I have confidence in You for not just one or two things but for *all* things. I trust that You have a plan for me. That You will answer my call if ever I'm in trouble. That You will come to me and be with me in the *midst* of trouble. That You will never let me go. With You and me, Lord, it's personal. What love, what peace, what protection I have in You! Amen.

Day 107

THINK ON YOUR THOUGHTS

"For my thoughts are not your thoughts, neither are your ways my ways," declares the LORD. "As the heavens are higher than the earth, so are my ways higher than your ways and my thoughts than your thoughts."

ISAIAH 55:8–9

Lord, I'm sitting with Psalm 139 and the mind-blowing reality that You know my thoughts even before I do. This is cray-zee! Because, let's be honest, there are a lot of thoughts in this brain of mine. What's even more amazing is that You, the Maker of all, think about *me*.

So I'm curious, what *do* You think about me? What are Your thoughts toward me? How do You see me? What makes You laugh? What is entirely unique about how You formed my being? My soul? My passions? My story? I'm offering myself space to listen before I rush to think.

In place of my own thoughts, would You please allow me to peer into Your thoughts? To pay attention to where You are transforming and inviting me to surrender more deeply. May my thoughts be more aligned with Yours. I offer this discipline to You today and ask, "What do You think about me, Lord?" Amen.

Day 108
MIND OVER MATTERS

Keep your minds thinking about whatever is true, whatever is respected, whatever is right, whatever is pure, whatever can be loved, and whatever is well thought of. If there is anything good and worth giving thanks for, think about these things. Keep on doing all the things you learned and received and heard from me. Do the things you saw me do. Then the God Who gives peace will be with you.
PHILIPPIANS 4:8–9 NLV

Too often, Lord, I find myself so engrossed in the bad things happening in the world that I forget about all the good that surrounds me—You and Your Word included. Help me lift my thoughts in Your direction, Lord. I want to fill my mind and meditate on things that are good, true, and uplifting. I want to think the best, not the worst; of the lovely, not the unlovely. I want to think of things to praise, not things to criticize. But I need Your help. Make it my desire, Lord, to fill my mind with You before I reach for the paper or turn on the news. For I know that if I'm full of You and Your goodness, I won't have room for anything else—but joy. Amen.

Day 109

FREEDOM

It is for freedom that Christ has set us free.
Stand firm, then, and do not let yourselves be
burdened again by a yoke of slavery.
GALATIANS 5:1

Jesus, You have set me free! I feel renewed and refreshed since I've started living my life for You. Before, I lived for myself and fulfilling all my selfish wants. I thought I was free in the belief that I could do whatever made me happy, but I felt so empty. And truly I wasn't free at all. I was bound in the chains of sin, controlled by my desire. I was living in a gilded prison of my own making. But You showed me a different way, Jesus! Now I am truly free from a load of guilt and satisfied by Your living water. Following You is my new purpose. Becoming a slave to righteousness has set me free. In the name of Jesus, amen.

Day 110

GREAT THINGS AWAIT

"Do not be distressed or angry with yourselves because you sold me here, for God sent me before you to preserve life. . . . God sent me before you. . .to keep alive for you many survivors. So it was not you who sent me here, but God. He has made me a father to Pharaoh, and lord of all his house and ruler over all the land of Egypt."
GENESIS 45:5, 7–8 ESV

When I'm lying awake at night wondering, *Why me?* or *What did I do to deserve this?* I inevitably come back to Joseph. All the things that he'd been through—sold to slave traders by his brothers, unjustly accused of a crime, thrown into a dungeon, then forgotten and neglected—would be enough to crush such a dreamer, to turn his stomach into a knot of anxiety and frustration. Instead, Joseph stuck with God, stayed calm, and carried on, continually going on to the next thing, knowing that God was in control and that great things awaited him! That's how I want to be, Lord. As calm, cool, and collected as Joseph, during good times and bad. Amen.

Day 111

SOURCE OF ALL LOVE

Whoever does not love does not know
God, because God is love.
1 John 4:8

You are the source of all love. Anything that reflects love, is in love, or creates love is Yours, God. Love is fullness of light and wonder and beauty. In You there is no darkness or heaviness or shame.

Where do I see love in me? Where am I living through Your love and living loved as a result? Where am I carrying darkness that isn't mine to carry? Forgive me for paying more attention to the existence of darkness rather than walking confidently in the light.

Lord, my heart cry is this: Where and how can I step fully into Your love today? Where do I resist Your love? Why? Where do I have a hard time allowing all of me to be loved? What's this about? Where do I readily receive Your love? May I bask in the light of Your love and not feel pressure to do anything with it other than humbly receive. Amen.

Day 112

GLAD IN GOD

I'm glad in God, far happier than you would ever guess. . . . I don't have a sense of needing anything personally. I've learned by now to be quite content whatever my circumstances. I'm just as happy with little as with much, with much as with little. I've found the recipe for being happy whether full or hungry, hands full or hands empty. Whatever I have, wherever I am, I can make it through anything in the One who makes me who I am.
PHILIPPIANS 4:10–13 MSG

So many people are miserable, Lord. They are always in a state of wanting, never quite feeling complete and happy. I must admit that sometimes I find myself there too. I am envious of others and what they have and can do. But then I think of You and all those desires fade. I find myself quite content, even happy with what I have and what's happening in my life, for You, Lord, are all I need. With You giving me strength, grace, mercy, love, hope, and so much more, I'm happy whether my pantry is full or empty, my house warm or cold, my bank balance overflowing or sparse. I'm at peace and glad in You. Amen.

Day 113
HE GUIDES ME

*Trust in the Lord with all your heart and lean not
on your own understanding; in all your ways submit
to him, and he will make your paths straight.*
PROVERBS 3:5–6

Father, making decisions can be so confusing. Sometimes I don't know which way to turn. Navigating the fog of this world disorients me. Thank You for always being my guidance system. I trust You and Your Word above my own feeble attempts to understand all the threads You are weaving together in Your master plan. Jesus, I submit my life to You. And because I have laid all my decisions before You and asked for Your wisdom, I know that You will steady my course. I won't run aground in the murky waters of this life because You are my lighthouse. You are the blazing beacon that guides me through the darkness into right choices. In Your name, Jesus, amen.

Day 114
NOTHING LOST

Jesus then took the loaves, and when he had given thanks, he distributed them to those who were seated. So also the fish, as much as they wanted. And when they had eaten their fill, he told his disciples, "Gather up the leftover fragments, that nothing may be lost." So they gathered them up and filled twelve baskets with fragments from the five barley loaves left by those who had eaten.
JOHN 6:11–13 ESV

Lord, You are continually amazing me with Your power, wisdom, and creativity, all of which shine through the stories in Your Word. Each day, I reach for Your Book and find a new lesson, a new treasure, a new phrase that draws me closer to knowing You. Today I'm reminded of how well You provide for me, how prayers and faith move me in the telling and doing, and then move You to provide a miracle, to go beyond a point I thought unreachable. Today I find my peace knowing that You, Lord, are the ultimate provider, the God of wonder, the Spirit of light. Thank You for never allowing anything to be lost. Even me. Amen.

Day 115

SPIRIT DISCERNMENT

For the word of God is living and active, sharper
than any two-edged sword, piercing to the division
of soul and of spirit, of joints and of marrow, and
discerning the thoughts and intentions of the heart.
HEBREWS 4:12 ESV

God, I feel full of anticipation. I sense You are moving me forward, but to what I'm not sure. When this happens, I feel doubt creep in. Do You really care? Do You see me? Do You really have big plans for me?

Much of my journey is one of slowing down and listening to Your voice, and I sense that tension of wanting to perform and simultaneously desiring to be still and small. How do I do both well? Please give me discernment and help me stay where Your peace is, where Your discerning presence is, where You are moving me toward a path everlasting.

Anything that distracts, threatens, or interrupts this space is not of You. Please give me awareness to turn and continue walking confidently toward Your grace. Forgive me, Lord, when I stay in my head and lose sight of Your work in me and through others. I ask for Spirit discernment today. In Jesus' name, amen.

Day 116

A QUIET STRENGTH

*Blessed (happy, blithesome, joyous, spiritually prosperous—
with life-joy and satisfaction in God's favor and salvation,
regardless of their outward conditions) are the meek (the
mild, patient, long-suffering), for they shall inherit the
earth!... Say to the Daughter of Zion..., Behold, your
King is coming to you, lowly and riding on a donkey, and
on a colt, the foal of a donkey [a beast of burden].*
MATTHEW 5:5; 21:5 AMPC

When I think about it, it doesn't seem like I'd be very happy
being meek, Jesus. Yet that is what You were and what You've
called me to be. When I look to You as my example, I realize
being meek doesn't mean being weak. It means being obedient
to Abba God. Trusting Him to handle what I cannot. Being quiet
and patient while He works out His will and way. And being gentle with others. In this view, being meek carries strength with it.
You Yourself, the Son of God and my King, rode a simple donkey through the throng the Sunday before Your death. I want
to have that meekness, that trust in Abba God. Show me the
way there so that I too can find the joy that comes with quiet
strength. Amen.

Day 117

A BETTER HOPE

For the law never made anything perfect.
But now we have confidence in a better hope,
through which we draw near to God.
HEBREWS 7:19 NLT

Heavenly Father, thank You for sending Jesus to provide us with a better hope of being close to You. You knew that the Law would not save us fallible humans. We can't help but mess up and break the rules, sometimes a lot. Failure seems to be our default setting, and no matter how hard we try, our efforts to achieve righteousness through the Law are feeble and steeped in failure. But then You sent us Jesus and rent the curtain that prevented our entry into Your inner sanctuary. Now we have a better way to draw near to You. Instead of following rules, we can have a personal relationship with You, Father. We can know You and be known by You. In Jesus' name, amen.

Day 118
THE RIGHT SHORE

They saw Jesus walking on the sea and approaching the boat. And they were afraid (terrified). But Jesus said to them, It is I; be not afraid! [I Am; stop being frightened!] Then they were quite willing and glad for Him to come into the boat. And now the boat went at once to the land they had steered toward. [And immediately they reached the shore toward which they had been slowly making their way.]
JOHN 6:19–21 AMPC

Sometimes, Lord, I wonder why I'm getting nowhere with a project, task, challenge, or situation. I feel as if I'm out on a stormy sea, unable to see past the wind and waves, that all my rowing, all my efforts to move things forward are coming to naught. And then I realize I haven't invited You into my plans. For some reason, I've left You out of my equation. So here I am, Lord, letting You into my plan. Here's what I'm steering toward. Now that we're together on this, I can ride on in peace and make my way to the right shore with You. Amen.

Day 119
NOTICING THE GIFT OF QUIET

*"The LORD your God is in your midst, a mighty one who will
save; he will rejoice over you with gladness; he will quiet
you by his love; he will exult over you with loud singing."*
ZEPHANIAH 3:17 ESV

Lord, when I pause and surrender to stillness and quiet, what
are You saying? Do I make time to listen to Your voice? I admit,
many times I take Your quietness for distance. I associate quietness with my own experience: people are quiet when they are
mad, when they are acting passive-aggressively, when they are
uncomfortable. I experience quietness from others, and their
quietness feels heavy.

Your quietness though, Lord, is light. And safe. And flowing
with peace. As You invite me to sit in Your quiet and familiarize
myself with Your stillness, help me pay attention to the peace I
experience. In Your quiet, there is no angry silence or passive-
aggressive energy or intentional ignoring.

What are You offering in Your quiet? I will sit and listen and
find comfort in being with You now. Amen.

Day 120

SPIRITUAL NOURISHMENT

He opened His mouth and taught them, saying. . . .
Blessed and fortunate and happy and spiritually
prosperous (in that state in which the born-again child of
God enjoys His favor and salvation) are those who hunger
and thirst for righteousness (uprightness and right standing
with God), for they shall be completely satisfied! . . .
The disciples urged Him saying, Rabbi, eat something.
But He assured them, I have food (nourishment) to
eat of which you know nothing and have no idea.
MATTHEW 5:2, 6; JOHN 4:31–32 AMPC

Abba God, only You can fill this longing I have inside, this God-shaped hole within me. I ache to hear Your voice, see Your face, feel Your touch. I hunger and thirst for all You have to give me, for all You are holding for me. I know You're just waiting to give me everything I need. So help me, Lord, to let go of all things that are not of You—worries, fears, and what-ifs; possessions, deadlines, stress, and anxieties. For when I empty myself of all but You and Your Word, I know I'll find the nourishment that brings with it all the joy my spirit craves. Amen.

Day 121

A SOLID FOUNDATION

*"Such is the destiny of all who forget God; so perishes
the hope of the godless. What they trust in is fragile;
what they rely on is a spider's web. They lean on the web,
but it gives way; they cling to it, but it does not hold."*
JOB 8:13–15

God, I choose to place my hope in You. I choose to discipline my mind to filter out the messages of discouragement and despair and fear that assault me when the storms of life rage against me. When my circumstances look dark, I will continue walking toward the light. I won't forget You in troubled times, because I have faith in Your almighty sovereignty, Father. And I know that my faith is not misplaced. I can lean on You without fear that You will collapse beneath the load like a fragile spider's web. You are a rock, firm and solid for my foundation. My faith in You gives me hope of new life, a changed heart, and eternity. In the name of Jesus, amen.

Day 122
LIVE CAREFREE

All of you, leaders and followers alike, are to be down to earth with each other, for—God has had it with the proud, but takes delight in just plain people. So be content with who you are, and don't put on airs. God's strong hand is on you; he'll promote you at the right time. Live carefree before God; he is most careful with you.
1 PETER 5:5–7 MSG

Lord, I want to be down-to-earth, talking straight not only to other humans but to You too. But I'll need Your help. Please give me the courage to tell You everything that's happening in my life; the things I've thought, said, and done; the good, the bad, and the ugly. I want not just to be satisfied, content with who I am, but to be assured that You too are content, perhaps even happy, with who I am or the woman I'm working toward being. But most of all, Lord, I want to turn over to You *all* the things that are bothering me, give You *all* my burdens, my fumes and frets, and leave them in Your more than capable hands. In Jesus' name, amen.

Day 123

INTENTIONAL PURPOSE

The plans of the diligent lead surely to abundance,
but everyone who is hasty comes only to poverty.
PROVERBS 21:5 ESV

I'm a busy soul. I leave no margin for rest or breathing room on either side of my full calendar. Forgive me, God, for I feel in my body that this is not healthy. When I'm late, I become crabby and resentful and angry. I am mad at. . . ? Who? Only I am in charge of my schedule! Here lies my challenge. I'm planning too much and frustrated when I'm exhausted at the end of the day.

Where are You inviting me to plan and live and create intentional space to breathe? Where am I scheduling time to be in Your presence? Am I blowing up the box I have You in and living open to how You breathe life into everyday, mundane tasks? In the cleaning and errands and driving, You are here.

Please help me not to waste another moment rushing frantically from one task to the next, but to live with intent and mindful awareness that You are with me in all parts of my day. In Jesus' name, amen.

Day 124
REVIVED AGAIN

Be to me a rock of refuge, to which I may continually come. . . . O God, from my youth you have taught me, and I still proclaim your wondrous deeds. So even to old age and gray hairs, O God, do not forsake me, until I proclaim your might to another generation. . . . You. . .will revive me again. . . . My lips will shout for joy, when I sing praises to you.
PSALM 71:3, 17–18, 20, 23 ESV

You have never failed me, Lord. When I've needed Your help, You have always come through for me. Time and time again, You have worked wonders in my life. Since I was a child in the faith, You have been my rock of refuge. So do not leave me now, Lord. Help me to grow more and more like Your Son, Jesus. Give me the words to tell others of Your power, love, compassion, and strength. Renew me. Fill me with Your light. Work in me for Your good and glory. And I will shout for joy as I sing Your praises for Your glory. Amen.

Day 125

THE HOPE OF HEAVEN

And if Christ has not been raised, then your faith is useless and you are still guilty of your sins. In that case, all who have died believing in Christ are lost! And if our hope in Christ is only for this life, we are more to be pitied than anyone in the world.
1 Corinthians 15:17–19 NLT

Father God, how pointless and hopeless our lives would be if this world was all there was to look forward to. What hope and joy would we have if the short span of our years here winked out with our final breath and then there was nothing—no glorious streets of gold, no eternity with You and our loved ones in Christ, no greater purpose for our existence than our own selfish ambitions? Without You, we would have no forgiveness or hope of redemption. But You have given us a new hope. The promise of more. The promise of being with You in a perfect place where pain and sin no longer exist. You have given us forever. In Jesus' name, amen.

Day 126
EVEN BETTER

Fear not, for I have redeemed you [ransomed you by paying a price instead of leaving you captives]; I have called you by your name; you are Mine. When you pass through the waters, I will be with you, and through the rivers, they will not overwhelm you. When you walk through the fire, you will not be burned or scorched, nor will the flame kindle upon you. For I am the Lord your God, the Holy One of Israel, your Savior.
ISAIAH 43:1–3 AMPC

Oh Lord, You give me such peace of mind. When I am afraid, You tell me to "fear not" because You've redeemed me, even though it cost the sacrifice of Your Child. And You continue to reach out for me, willing and longing to help me. You've even called me by name, claiming ownership of me—mind, body, and soul. Even better, You've promised to stick with me through times of fire and times of rain. And all because You love me, all because You want me in Your world, Your presence. Alleluia, amen!

Day 127

THE ULTIMATE ANSWER

*From heaven the L*ORD *looks down and sees all mankind; from his dwelling place he watches all who live on earth—he who forms the hearts of all, who considers everything they do.*
PSALM 33:13–15

God, I don't get it. I don't understand what's happening in this season. Forgive me for feeling like I need to understand everything. I don't need to have all the answers, but to look to You as the ultimate answer.

Why do I struggle with needing to understand and make sense and know? What's simmering beneath this? Forgive me, Lord, for making understanding an idol, one I worship more than the messy process of trusting You one moment at a time. Your ways are perfect. Help me trust this truth. Help me settle into knowing that You know all things. You understand everything. You have the full picture. You get it. Through and through. When I panic at my lack of understanding, would You please pull my face to Yours and whisper, "I have you. And My understanding is enough and perfect and good. I've got you."

Thank You, Jesus. Amen.

Day 128
NEVER FORGOTTEN

Sing for joy, O heavens! Be glad, O earth! Break out into songs of joy, O mountains! For the Lord has comforted His people. . . . "Can a woman forget her nursing child? Can she have no pity on the son to whom she gave birth? Even these may forget, but I will not forget you. See, I have marked your names on My hands. Your walls are always before Me."
ISAIAH 49:13, 15–16 NLV

Oh Lord, with You in my life, I need not worry about being passed over! For You are always with me. You will never forget me—just like a nursing mother will never forget her newborn. But You go even further by tattooing my name on Your hands! Thank You for leading me, protecting me before and behind, providing for me, healing me, showering me with blessings, and fighting those who threaten me. Your pervading presence in my life gives me such joy. Such peace of mind. You chase all my blues away. Thank You, Father God, for never leaving me behind. Because of You, I break out singing songs of joy. In Jesus' name, I praise You. Amen.

Day 129

GOD OF ALL COMFORT

*Praise be to the God and Father of our Lord Jesus Christ,
the Father of compassion and the God of all comfort, who
comforts us in all our troubles, so that we can comfort
those in any trouble with the comfort we ourselves receive
from God. For just as we share abundantly in the sufferings
of Christ, so also our comfort abounds through Christ.*
2 Corinthians 1:3–5

Father, You aren't a distant God who is unmoved by my pain and
struggles. You don't remove Yourself from my messy situations.
Instead You step into the middle of my upturned life with compassion and comfort. You soothe my worries and bind up my
broken heart. While I might suffer as Jesus did in this world, You
minister tenderly to me like the great Shepherd that You are.
How wonderful to have a God that I can turn to when I need
a hug, when I'm overwhelmed, when I hurt. You shower me in
comfort through my hope in Jesus. And now I can take the comfort You have shown me and offer it to those around me. In the
name of Jesus, amen.

Day 130

THE SECRET OF FACING EVERY SITUATION

Not that I am implying that I was in any personal want, for I have learned how to be content (satisfied to the point where I am not disturbed or disquieted) in whatever state I am. I know how to be abased and live humbly in straitened circumstances, and I know also how to enjoy plenty and live in abundance. I have learned in any and all circumstances the secret of facing every situation.
PHILIPPIANS 4:11–12 AMPC

Help me get it through my head, Lord, that I, by myself, cannot meet my own needs. That only through You can I find the true contentment, joy, and peace I crave. Instead of trying to come up with my own solutions or thinking I know better than You, I'm going to trust You for everything—big and small. I'm going to allow You into every facet of my life. And I'm going to be satisfied with who I am, what I have, and where I am as I keep my eyes on You. I know You do all things well and in Your own time. In You, I am content with all. Amen.

Day 131
EVER-PRESENT SPIRIT

And he said to them, "Pay attention to what you hear: with the measure you use, it will be measured to you, and still more will be added to you."
MARK 4:24 ESV

God, sometimes I forget to notice that You are always with me. When I am sad, You are with me. Joyful? You are with me. You tell me that if I go to the heavens, You are there. And to the depths of the earth, You are still with me. I love that You are a constant companion, a friend as well as my Savior.

God, please forgive me for neglecting this truth. For mistaking Your intimacy for a feeling. You are with me even when I can't feel You. Even when I'm walking through the valley, Your Spirit is ever present. I'm quieting myself now to listen. Help me notice the movement of Your Spirit in this moment. In this day. In my comings and goings and thoughts and questions. Awaken me to how personal and near and constant Your Spirit is in and through me.

I'm so grateful that You are a God I don't have to go to. You draw near and stay with me through every moment. Amen.

Day 132
PURE LIGHT AND JOY

You are the Lord Most High over all the earth. . . . Let those who love the Lord hate what is bad. For He keeps safe the souls of His faithful ones. He takes them away from the hand of the sinful. Light is spread like seed for those who are right and good, and joy for the pure in heart. Be glad in the Lord, you who are right and good. Give thanks to His holy name.
PSALM 97:9–12 NLV

Lord, help my love of You to keep me away from things that are not good for me. Anything that is not good is not of You, God. Keep my soul safe from the evil that presents itself in the physical and spiritual worlds. Hide me under Your banner of love so that the sinful cannot reach me. Shine Your light along my way so that I will not stumble upon Your path. Help me to continue to walk in Jesus' steps, the right and good way, for there alone will I find the deep joy I seek and the pure love I crave from You. In Jesus' name, I pray. Amen.

Day 133
REFRESHMENT

"The LORD is my strength and my defense; he has become my salvation. He is my God, and I will praise him, my father's God, and I will exalt him."
EXODUS 15:2

Father, by the end of each day, I'm ready to collapse. I'm exhausted both physically and spiritually by family life, work, and worry. But how comforting and uplifting to know that I can renew my strength from Your fountain that is ever flowing. Your strength never runs dry. You replenish my soul. In the midst of my daily struggle, it's so easy to be distracted from the promises of Your Word. Sometimes I fail You and fall to temptation. Remind me of Your faithfulness to those who believe. Remind me of Your deep love for me. Remind me that I have hope in Jesus, who came to save me. And this world is not my final home. In Jesus' name, amen.

Day 134
GOD'S PLANNING

*Joseph replied, "Don't be afraid. Do I act for God?
Don't you see, you planned evil against me but God used
those same plans for my good, as you see all around
you right now—life for many people. Easy now, you have
nothing to fear; I'll take care of you and your children."
He reassured them, speaking with them heart-to-heart.*
GENESIS 50:19–21 MSG

Lord, the news—local and international—is full of reports of people acting from their worst instincts and ideas. Such events are more than unsettling. Yet this behavior, people hurting people, has been happening for thousands of years, hasn't it? Still, I cannot get used to it. When others hurt, so do I. We're all connected, all Your people. So, Lord, help me gain some peace about this. Give me the courage to adopt Joseph's attitude—to remember that even while others plan evil, You can use those same plans for my good and the good of others. Because that's what You do, I know I really have nothing to fear, nothing to worry about, no reason to hold a grudge. Ah, that's how I find peace—Your peace as You turn evil into good. Thank God! Amen.

Day 135
THIS PAUSE

I believe that I shall look upon the goodness of the Lord in the land of the living! Wait for the Lord; be strong, and let your heart take courage; wait for the Lord!
PSALM 27:13–14 ESV

God, I feel like life is on pause. There's little movement or direction. I'm listening but unsure of how to move forward or what to lean into. What happens in this pause? Fear. Anxiety. I can feel my blood pressure skyrocket and am tempted to kick into "go mode" simply to make any type of action occur.

Why do I do this? What scares me about being on pause? Please forgive me, Lord, for my impatience. What are You inviting me to notice, learn, or surrender in this in-between place? Where are You asking me to stay when I really just want to crawl out of my skin and make something happen?

Perhaps, Lord, the purpose of this pause isn't the next step but a greater intimacy with knowing You are here. You are in the middle of the "not yet." You are in control of this pause, and for this reason alone I trust You. Amen.

Day 136
OPEN DOORS

Though the disciples were behind closed doors for fear of the Jews, Jesus came and stood among them and said, Peace to you! So saying, He showed them His hands and His side. And when the disciples saw the Lord, they were filled with joy (delight, exultation, ecstasy, rapture). Then Jesus said to them again, Peace to you! . . . And having said this, He breathed on them and said to them, Receive the Holy Spirit!
JOHN 20:19–22 AMPC

Lord Jesus, sometimes this world leaves me cowering in fear, afraid to move forward. In defense, I put up walls and barriers, hoping my safety will lie there. But You, Lord, open all doors and come shining through. Your words and Your blessing of peace draw me out of my fear and into You. Seeing Your face, I am filled with joy once more. Reminded of who You are, what You've suffered for me, I am renewed, made whole again. Your peace and Spirit surround me, cocooning me in Your grace, mercy, love, and presence. Breathe on me, Jesus. Strengthen my heart, soul, and mind as I abide and rest in You. Amen.

Day 137
A FOREVER HOME

*For this world is not our permanent home; we are
looking forward to a home yet to come. Therefore,
let us offer through Jesus a continual sacrifice of praise
to God, proclaiming our allegiance to his name.*
HEBREWS 13:14–15 NLT

God, don't allow me to get too comfortable here. When I do, I start enjoying the pleasures and comforts of life a little too much. My eyes wander to the things I can build for myself and the possessions I can accumulate. My efforts stray from building Your kingdom to building my own little empire here in this world. But this place doesn't last. Peter told Your followers to live as strangers in this world, pilgrims who are just passing through. Remind me to keep my bags packed for heaven, that there's a better place I'm waiting for. Right now I'm merely in the prelude to my eternity with You. I live in hopeful anticipation of that forever city. In Jesus' name, amen.

Day 138
PEACE OF KNOWLEDGE

*I have learned in any and all circumstances the secret of
facing every situation, whether well-fed or going hungry,
having a sufficiency and enough to spare or going without
and being in want. I have strength for all things in Christ
Who empowers me [I am ready for anything and equal
to anything through Him Who infuses inner strength
into me; I am self-sufficient in Christ's sufficiency].*
PHILIPPIANS 4:12–13 AMPC

No matter what's happening in my life, Lord, I know that because of You, I'll never want for anything. For I belong to You,
the master Creator, maintainer, and sustainer of all things. And
because I'm Yours, everything I see around me reminds me of
You, Your power, Your beauty, and Your love. All I have, want,
and require is in You, from You, and through You. Because I live
in You and Your Son, I have it all, including strength to do, think,
or say what You would have me do, think, or say. Through Your
Son, I'm ready for anything because He is my everything, my
security, strength, and peace. In Jesus' name, amen.

Day 139

CHOSEN TODAY AND EVERY DAY

As you come to him, a living stone rejected by men but in the sight of God chosen and precious, you yourselves like living stones are being built up as a spiritual house, to be a holy priesthood, to offer spiritual sacrifices acceptable to God through Jesus Christ.
1 PETER 2:4–5 ESV

God, I feel rejected. Unchosen. Invisible. Like the kid who didn't get picked on the playground. Did You ever feel this way? You were rejected by Your hometown. The very people You grew up with tried to run You out. And my heart simultaneously breaks and finds comfort in knowing You understand.

Rejection is painful. But please help me not lose myself to shame. Forgive me for even entertaining the thought that because I've been rejected, I'm rejectable. This is not the truth. This is not who I am or how You see me. I am chosen by You.

Please forgive me for assuming there's a flaw in me, a reason for this rejection. Turn my heart to the truth that perhaps You are protecting me in this circumstance. You are teaching me compassion. You are reminding me that, regardless of being chosen or unchosen, I am fearfully and wonderfully made. In Jesus' name, amen.

Day 140
BLESSINGS OF GOODNESS

The king shall have joy in Your strength, O LORD; and in Your salvation how greatly shall he rejoice! You have given him his heart's desire, and have not withheld the request of his lips. For You meet him with the blessings of goodness. . . . You have made him exceedingly glad with Your presence. For the king trusts in the LORD, and through the mercy of the Most High he shall not be moved.
PSALM 21:1–3, 6–7 NKJV

It's Your strength and power, Lord, that get me through each day and bring me great joy. Every day, You shower me with blessings, giving me what I desire, answering my prayers. All that is good comes from Your hand. And for all these things, I thank You, Lord. Yet no blessing, no good thing You place in my life, gives me more joy than Your very presence. It is my trust that You will come when I call, my faith that You are here by my side right now, and my belief in Your loving-kindness that keeps me steady, able to walk, able to serve You. In Jesus' name, amen.

Day 141
REDEEMED

For you know that it was not with perishable things such as silver or gold that you were redeemed from the empty way of life handed down to you from your ancestors, but with the precious blood of Christ, a lamb without blemish or defect. He was chosen before the creation of the world, but was revealed in these last times for your sake.
1 PETER 1:18–20

Lord Jesus, the habits of sin can be so difficult to break. I think I'm maturing in my walk, and suddenly I'm blindsided by another misstep. I repeat a cycle of sin I thought I left behind. I disappoint You, and I stumble. I fall hard on my face. But then I look up and see Your nail-pierced hand held out to me. I take it and stand again because You have redeemed me from that empty way of life. For my sake You died, a perfect and unblemished sacrifice to free me from my bonds of sin. Even when I falter, I'm no longer ensnared by my old attitudes and actions, because I'm redeemed. I'm bought by Your blood, and I belong to You. Amen.

Day 142
A GOOD PLACE

I cried to the Lord in my trouble, and He answered me and put me in a good place. The Lord is with me. I will not be afraid of what man can do to me. The Lord is with me. He is my Helper. I will watch those lose who fight against me. It is better to trust in the Lord than to trust in man. It is better to trust in the Lord than to trust in rulers.
PSALM 118:5–9 NLV

God, You are not just "my strength and my song" (Psalm 118:14 NLV); You are my peace. You are the one who calms my racing heart, caresses my weary brow, and holds my shaking hand. Whenever I'm in trouble, You hear my call. You realize what's happening, answer my SOS, lift me up, and put me in a good place—a place where You are. When You are with me, Lord, I'm not afraid. When You are with me, when I'm conscious of Your presence, I realize I have all I need. Unlike humans, You can be trusted, Lord. With and in You, I find my good place. Amen.

Day 143
STILL GOOD

Lord, by such things people live; and my spirit finds
life in them too. You restored me to health and let
me live. Surely it was for my benefit that I suffered
such anguish. In your love you kept me from the pit of
destruction; you have put all my sins behind your back.
ISAIAH 38:16–17

I've been thinking lately about healing. About how we, as believers, pray for healing. What about the times when healing isn't on this side of heaven? Is that still *healing*? What is *true* healing? God, I confess I selfishly pray for people to be healed. For suffering to end. For illnesses to disappear. For cancer to be erased. Why do horrible diseases and tragedies happen? Where are You in these circumstances?

I bring these honest questions to You and trust You can handle them. Know my heart, Lord, and please draw me to find security in You alone. God, perhaps my prayer for healing is an invitation to find my longings fulfilled in eternity with You, where there is no sickness. Until then, please give me boldness to pray and trust that You heal in out-of-the-box ways. I don't always have to understand to know that You are still good. Amen.

Day 144
PURE HEART VISION

*He opened His mouth and taught them, saying. . .
Blessed (happy, enviably fortunate, and spiritually
prosperous. . .) are the pure in heart, for they shall see
God! . . . No man has ever seen God at any time; the
only unique Son. . .Who is in the bosom [in the intimate
presence] of the Father, He has declared Him [He has
revealed Him and brought Him out where He can be seen].*
MATTHEW 5:2, 8; JOHN 1:18 AMPC

Only by looking at and through You, Jesus, can I see God in all His goodness, strength, power, mercy, and loving-kindness. Yet to be able to see God completely, to actually be able to fully enter into His presence, my heart and mind must be right with You. So help me, Lord, to get and keep my heart pure. Help me focus my thoughts on You, Jesus, and steep myself in Your Word. I want to walk in Your way. To stay on Your path. To forgive as You have forgiven. And to follow Your lead in all I do and say, all I think and pray. In Your name, amen.

Day 145
DRAW NEAR

He gives us more grace. That is why Scripture says: "God opposes the proud but shows favor to the humble." Submit yourselves, then, to God. Resist the devil, and he will flee from you. Come near to God and he will come near to you.

JAMES 4:6–8

Father, *submit* and *humble* are two words I cringe at reading in Your Word. Just like running into a coffee table in the dark, I've cracked the battered shins of my soul against the hard edge of my pride on numerous occasions. But You give grace generously to the humble. I have hope that, through the power of Your Holy Spirit who dwells in me, I can learn to quell my pride. I submit myself to You, Lord. I will resist Satan's attempts to convince me that my wants and needs are more important than others'. Purify my heart. Show me the hidden stains of pride. Thank You, Father, that I can come closer to You and know that You will be there. Amen.

Day 146
RELAX

" 'Daniel,' he said, 'man of quality, listen carefully to my message. And get up on your feet. Stand at attention. I've been sent to bring you news.' When he had said this, I stood up, but I was still shaking. 'Relax, Daniel,' he continued, 'don't be afraid. From the moment you decided to humble yourself to receive understanding, your prayer was heard, and I set out to come to you.' "
DANIEL 10:11–12 MSG

I'm amazed, Lord, at how often You and Your angels tell me not to fear. Yet even faith-filled believers like Daniel sometimes shook with fright. I'm pretty certain I too would shake in fear if an angel came to visit me. So I'm feeling a bit better about the qualms that sometimes wiggle their way into my life, mind, and heart. Even so, it's good to hear the words *relax and don't be afraid*. It's nice to be reminded that You *answer* prayers and that You hear me when I call and then send an angel to help me. In this moment, Lord, open my ears to Your voice, my eyes to Your light, my heart to Your peace, and my spirit to Your angels. Amen.

Day 147

FLEXIBLE AND TEACHABLE

I know how to be brought low, and I know how to abound. In any and every circumstance, I have learned the secret of facing plenty and hunger, abundance and need. I can do all things through him who strengthens me. Yet it was kind of you to share my trouble.
PHILIPPIANS 4:12–14 ESV

God, nothing is going as planned. Health. House emergencies. A change in work plans. When I find myself clinging to control and order, would You redirect me to notice how I can be flexible and teachable instead? Where do I need to surrender my plan for Yours?

Please forgive me for focusing on getting things done and neglecting to sit with You first. None of this comes as a surprise. I confess I don't need You until I do. And I need You now.

May my daily prayer be *God, I begin this day with intent. I trust that as I work and listen and hold my hands open in expectancy, You will not let me miss anything. May my focus be You and You alone. Help me laugh when disruptions come and lean deeper into allowing small details to be just that: small. Amen.*

Day 148

AN EDEN–LIKE TRANSFORMATION

*"All you who are serious about right living and committed
to seeking G*OD*. Ponder the rock from which you were
cut. . . . Abraham, your father, and Sarah, who bore
you. Think of it! One solitary man when I called him,
but once I blessed him, he multiplied. Likewise I, G*OD*,
will comfort Zion. . . . I'll transform her dead ground into
Eden. . .the garden of G*OD*, a place filled with exuberance
and laughter, thankful voices and melodic songs."*
ISAIAH 51:1–3 MSG

You, Lord God, can do anything. And You *will* do anything for
those serious about living the way You want them to live. For
those committed to seeking You each and every day. From
Abraham to Jesus, You have blessed Your people by fulfilling
their most ardent desires. I want to be as serious about living
right as Abraham was. I want to be as committed to seeking You
as Jesus was. Then You will turn my world—within and without—
into a garden of Eden, a place where laughter is heard, love is
spread, and prayers of gratitude roll off our lips. Transform me,
Lord. In Jesus' name, amen.

Day 149
HE SATISFIES

You, God, are my God, earnestly I seek you; I thirst for you, my whole being longs for you, in a dry and parched land where there is no water. I have seen you in the sanctuary and beheld your power and your glory. Because your love is better than life, my lips will glorify you. I will praise you as long as I live.
PSALM 63:1–4

Lord, this world can feel like a barren desert, offering nothing that will satisfy the longings of my soul. I have tried to fill myself up with its comforts and pleasures, but ultimately they leave me feeling empty and alone. Success is cold comfort when I'm struggling or hurting. Money is fleeting and lasts only for this lifetime. I was longing for something more. But then I found You, my God. You held out a cup of living water that saturated my desiccated soul with new life—everlasting life. And You love me. I have found the "more" that I was seeking. It's You. You have repaired my broken places and forgiven my sins. I can't stop praising You for how You have saved me. Amen.

Day 150
"RETURN TO ME"

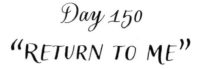

"I have made you, you are My servant. O Israel, I will not forget you. I have taken away your wrong-doing like a dark cloud, and your sins like a fog. Return to Me, for I have bought you and set you free."... The Lord, Who makes you, bought you and saves you, and the One Who put you together before you were born, says, "I am the Lord, Who made all things."
ISAIAH 44:21–22, 24 NLV

Some days, Lord, I'm amazed that You want me, that You want me to return to *You*. But You do! You've said that You, the one who has made me, will not forget me. That all the things I've done wrong, all the mistakes I've made—knowingly or unknowingly—You have taken away. They are no more. They're like a fog that's here then gone. Once more, I am amazed that You can obliterate my missteps like that. My one request today is that You help *me* forget my missteps and mistakes. Help me forgive myself for hurting You and anyone else who felt the results of my wrongdoing. Then, only then, will I have true peace in Jesus' name. Amen.

Day 151

HELP FOR HURTS

"The LORD will fight for you, and you have only to be silent."
EXODUS 14:14 ESV

I confess I feel shame in admitting that my feelings are hurt. A mocking voice says, "Get tough skin; stop being so sensitive." Yet, I would be lying to say I'm not hurt. And I need You to help me heal from this hurt before I can move on. To shove it deeper or ignore it would be to keep myself from feeling and healing. God, what is at the root of this hurt? What about this pain is my part to learn from? What part is not mine to carry and therefore necessary to grieve?

I'm handing You my hurt. Will You turn it over and reveal to me what to grow from and what to leave behind? Even as my heart is sad, please be my comfort. Thank You for listening and holding me and accepting all my big emotions and honest feelings. Thank You for loving me in this fragile space. Please cover me, Lord. I need Your safe arms right now. In Jesus' name, amen.

Day 152

RIGHT FOR LIFE

He began to teach them, saying, . . . "Those who have
it very hard for doing right are happy, because the holy
nation of heaven is theirs. You are happy when people act
and talk in a bad way to you and make it very hard for you
and tell bad things and lies about you because you trust
in Me." . . . [Christ] never sinned and yet He died for us
who have sinned. He died so He might bring us to God.
MATTHEW 5:2, 10–11; 1 PETER 3:18 NLV

Lord Jesus, there's no way I can ever repay You for all You've done for me. You who never sinned died so that I, a sinner, might live. You put up with the leers and jeers of the ungodly. You put up with the lies and the pain of unjust accusers. What You've gone through and done for me inspires me, Lord, to take this new life You've given me and live it for You—no matter what others say about me or do to me. As I live for You and trust in You, I gain Your kingdom of heaven—and all the joy and happiness that come with it. Thank You, Lord, for bringing me to God. In Your name, I pray, amen.

Day 153
HE SPEAKS TENDERLY

"She decked herself with rings and jewelry, and went after her lovers, but me she forgot," declares the LORD. "Therefore I am now going to allure her; I will lead her into the wilderness and speak tenderly to her. There I will give her back her vineyards, and will make the Valley of Achor a door of hope. There she will respond as in the days of her youth."
HOSEA 2:13–15

Father, I have chased after other loves in my life. I have cheated on Your great love for me with selfishness and deliberate disobedience. I have squandered time on myself and ignored Your requests. And yet, instead of berating me for my wrong choices and condemning me for my mistakes, You choose to woo me back to You with tender words. You take me into the desert so I can be alone with You. You are jealous of my affections and want my full attention. The desert may seem barren and lonely, but You are always near. You don't abandon me there, but rather You want me to praise You even in the wilderness. You are moving in my life even when I can't see You. Amen.

Day 154
THE STANDBY

I will ask the Father, and He will give you another Comforter (Counselor, Helper, Intercessor, Advocate, Strengthener, and Standby), that He may remain with you forever—the Spirit of Truth, Whom the world cannot receive (welcome, take to its heart), because it does not see Him or know and recognize Him. But you know and recognize Him, for He lives with you [constantly] and will be in you. I will not leave you as orphans.
JOHN 14:16–18 AMPC

Sometimes, Father, I feel just like an orphan, "comfortless, desolate, bereaved, forlorn, helpless" (John 14:18 AMPC). I've lost so many people in my life that I feel more alone than ever. I take comfort in the fact that the one-in-three person I have not lost and will never lose is You, Your Son, and Your Spirit. You have promised that Your Spirit will live with me forever. Your envoy will comfort, advise, help, intercede, advocate, strengthen, stand by me. He, that amazing Spirit of truth, is just the remedy I need to keep me from feeling all alone. He gives me peace of mind, heart, soul, and spirit. With all of You as my true and forever family, I am eternally blessed. In Jesus' name, amen.

Day 155
LIGHT IN THE DARKNESS

Again Jesus spoke to them, saying, "I am the light
of the world. Whoever follows me will not walk
in darkness, but will have the light of life."
JOHN 8:12 ESV

Anything that shimmers or hints of light is from You, Lord. Help me pay attention to this in my innermost being. Where is there peace? That's of You. Where is there joy? That's of You. Where is there a sense of feeling alive and whole? All of this beauty is from You.

I confess that I struggle to celebrate the light until it's dark. So I'm calling out my gratitude in the light and in the dark, for You are in all of it.

Where there is anxiety or lack of peace, help me turn toward Your light. Where there is shame or self-loathing, help me leave this behind. Where there is doubt and worry, let me lay this at Your feet. I only want to follow where You call my name and to believe this path is drenched in star-laden light. In Jesus' name, amen.

Day 156

LOOKING AT YOU

"O give thanks to the Lord. Call upon His name. Let the people know what He has done. Sing to Him. Sing praises to Him. Tell of all His great works. Have joy in His holy name. Let the heart of those who look to the Lord be glad. Look to the Lord and ask for His strength. Look to Him all the time. Remember His great works which He has done."
1 Chronicles 16:8–12 NLV

Today, Lord, I want to thank You for calling me. I praise Your name in remembrance of all You have done for Your people—from the parting of the Red Sea, to making the earth stand still, to sending a host of angels to protect us, to sending Your Son to bring us back to You, heart, body, mind, and soul. You have breathed Your life into me, Lord. And to You, my source, I look at all times—for guidance, protection, love, mercy, forgiveness, strength, and power. In Your name and works, in Your lovely face, I find all the joy I desire. Here's looking at You, Lord, today and forever. Amen.

Day 157

A NEW WAY OF THINKING

*Finally, brothers and sisters, whatever is true, whatever
is noble, whatever is right, whatever is pure, whatever is
lovely, whatever is admirable—if anything is excellent or
praiseworthy—think about such things. Whatever you have
learned or received or heard from me, or seen in me—put
it into practice. And the God of peace will be with you.*

PHILIPPIANS 4:8–9

Lord, I've been stuck in critical and judgmental thinking. Negative thoughts about myself and others swirl in my head. It makes me grumpy and unhappy when I allow unimportant stuff to bother me. But You have given me a solution, a new way of thinking. I choose to dwell on the positive. I will scour my surroundings for the true and lovely. I will focus on my husband's positive attributes instead of his flaws. I will praise my children when they're kind and loving instead of constantly chastising their mistakes. I will find the blessings stirred in with my unpleasant circumstances. Thank You, Jesus, for renewing my mind. Help me to practice what I have learned from You. In Jesus' name, amen.

Day 158
MOVING IN

*"I'm in my Father, and you're in me, and I'm in you.
The person who knows my commandments and keeps
them, that's who loves me. And the person who loves
me will be loved by my Father, and I will love him and
make myself plain to him. . . . If anyone loves me, he
will carefully keep my word and my Father will love
him—we'll move right into the neighborhood!"*
JOHN 14:20–21, 23 MSG

I have a sense of peace within me each time I think of You, Jesus. I feel so complete knowing You are in God, I'm in You, and You're in me. Because that means that no matter where I am or what I'm doing, I'm never alone. I always have someone with me who can give me wisdom, lift me up, shelter me from harm, and love me like no other. The last on that list is the most important, Lord, because this world can be such a loveless, unforgiving place. Fortunately for me, Lord, You loved me before I even knew You. That's a love to treasure, to count on, to rest in. Thank You. Amen.

Day 159
EVEN AS I WALK

*Dear friend, I pray that you may enjoy good
health and that all may go well with you,
even as your soul is getting along well.*
3 JOHN 2

God, as I walk up and down our street and notice the clouds and the birds and the flowers that are blooming and grass that is growing, may all of this be a whisper of Your creation. May I not pass by without noticing where You are seeding, uprooting, and showing Yourself in nature. God, thank You for the very legs that I walk on and my health. Forgive me for how easily I take this for granted. Even as I walk, will You strengthen my steps?

Continue to invite me forward to where You are growing me and tethering me deeper to Your Spirit and making me more discerning of Your voice. Thank You that You are a God who walks with, beside, behind, and in front of me. Thank You for hemming me in and companioning me right now, even as I walk. Amen.

Day 160

NEVER SEEN, YET BELIEVED

His disciples were again in the house, and Thomas was with them. Jesus came, though they were behind closed doors, and stood among them and said, Peace to you! . . . Because you have seen Me, Thomas, do you now believe (trust, have faith)? Blessed and happy and to be envied are those who have never seen Me and yet have believed and adhered to and trusted and relied on Me.
JOHN 20:26, 29 AMPC

It's true, Jesus. I have never seen You physically. Yet, unlike doubting Thomas, I believe in You. Between You and me are no closed doors. As soon as You stand beside me, I feel Your peace and joy, Your strength and power. You call me blessed and happy because I believe in, rely on, and trust in You without ever having seen You. And I *am!* You are my way to the Father. You are the truth I need. You are the life I seek. I am nowhere without You. So stick close to me, Lord, as I stick close to You. Continually bless me as I follow in Your footsteps. Help me to recognize that, no matter what each day brings, my path, my purpose, and my joy lie in You. Amen.

Day 161

A NEW KIND OF FRUIT

*But the fruit of the Spirit is love, joy, peace, forbearance,
kindness, goodness, faithfulness, gentleness and self-
control. Against such things there is no law. Those who
belong to Christ Jesus have crucified the flesh with
its passions and desires. Since we live by the Spirit,
let us keep in step with the Spirit. Let us not become
conceited, provoking and envying each other.*
GALATIANS 5:22–26

Jesus, since I met You, I'm living a new life—a life led by the
Holy Spirit. Instead of indulging whatever sinful urge enters my
mind, I'm following the direction of Your Spirit. And I'm seeing
the good results, the delicious evidence of the Spirit's work in
my life. Instead of the rottenness of anxiety and unhappiness,
I have tasted the sweetness of joy and peace and love. When I
am tempted toward anger, Your Spirit nudges me to patience.
When I want to lash out in spite when I'm slighted, I remember
Your kindness. Before, I thought the status quo was the only
way, now I know that I can nail my sinful nature to Your cross and
walk away. I can walk in step with Your Spirit. Amen.

Day 162
REPLENISH

Lift up your eyes on high and see! Who has created these? . . . Have you not known? Have you not heard? The everlasting God, the Lord, the Creator of the ends of the earth, does not faint or grow weary; there is no searching of His understanding. He gives power to the faint and weary, and to him who has no might He increases strength [causing it to multiply and making it to abound].
ISAIAH 40:26, 28–29 AMPC

I know who You are, Lord. You're the Creator of all. The one who holds, maintains, and sustains the entire world. I have known this. I had heard about it. But sometimes, almost unknowingly, I forget who You are. . .and, for that matter, who *I* am! I get so caught up in the day-to-day machinations in this world that I put You and Your power, strength, and knowledge to the side and tap into my resources alone. That's when I get into trouble. So here I am, Lord, faint and weary. Replenish me with Your peace, power, and strength. Shower me with Your wisdom, and help me keep my mind on You every moment of the day. Amen.

Day 163

RESPONDING WITH A YES OR NO

*"Let what you say be simply 'Yes' or 'No';
anything more than this comes from evil."*
MATTHEW 5:37 ESV

God, I notice my tendency to react instead of respond. To jump at the biggest need, the largest fire, and whoever is shouting the loudest. These needs are valid and important, yet it is not my job to be the rescuer or fix problems or provide for everyone's needs. Only You can do that.

I confess that often my identity comes from being the one who shows up, being the helper, having the right answer and the wise advice—and for this, I'm sorry. I'm sorry that my pride gets in the way.

Please be at the root of my responses. Stir me toward where You want me to say yes and where You want me to say no. May I stand courageously where You have me, where You want me to respond.

May I hold every need before You and think and pray and listen before I give an answer. I am thankful that You see all these needs. You know all these concerns. You hear every cry, and You are in all of this. In Jesus' name, amen.

Day 164
LIFTING UP

I will lift You up, O Lord, for You have lifted me up. You have not let those who hate me stand over me in joy. O Lord my God, I cried to You for help and You healed me. O Lord, You have brought me up from the grave. You have kept me alive, so that I will not go down into the deep. Sing praise to the Lord, all you who belong to Him. Give thanks to His holy name.
PSALM 30:1–4 NLV

It's only right that I should lift You up, Lord, because You've certainly lifted me up. When I first awoke, I wondered what this day would bring. But before my thoughts went too far, I looked to You and into Your Word. There I found how You continually help and heal me. You give me new life each and every day. You and Your light are what keep me from sliding into that dark abyss. So, today, Lord, I'm praising Your name, singing songs of love to You. I thank You for always being there, rescuing me when I'm in danger, walking with me through the storms, holding me tight in the night hours, showing me the pathway of life. . .in You. Amen.

Day 165
HE IS PATIENT

But do not forget this one thing, dear friends:
With the Lord a day is like a thousand years, and a
thousand years are like a day. The Lord is not slow in
keeping his promise, as some understand slowness.
Instead he is patient with you, not wanting anyone
to perish, but everyone to come to repentance.
2 PETER 3:8–9

God, Your amazing capacity for patience gives me great hope. Waiting is never easy. I always want to speed things up and have everything now, now, now. But You have the ability to wait for Your plans to work. You wait for the seeds sown in my life to take root and grow into maturity. You don't expect overnight growth. Instead You keep watering those seeds and feeding them until one day they sprout. You gently and patiently teach me with kindness. You love us enough to wait for us to come to You in repentance. You don't want to lose any of us. The answer to why You don't just return right now and stop this messed-up world is love and patience. In Jesus' name, amen.

Day 166
WITHIN ME

Peace I leave with you; My [own] peace I now give and bequeath to you. Not as the world gives do I give to you. Do not let your hearts be troubled, neither let them be afraid. [Stop allowing yourselves to be agitated and disturbed; and do not permit yourselves to be fearful and intimidated and cowardly and unsettled.]

JOHN 14:27 AMPC

It's strange reading the sentence "Stop allowing yourselves to be agitated and disturbed; and do not permit yourselves to be fearful," for I rarely consider that I have control over these things. And yet I do. I have a choice to make. I can allow the events of my day and my reactions to them to break my peace or not. I choose: not. But I will need Your help, Lord, to hang on to Your peace. The one You left with me. The very peace You carried, have given to, and bequeathed to me. To hang on to Your peace, I'm going to spend more time in You, with You, attending to You, beginning today by reminding myself over and over again that the God of peace is within me. Amen.

Day 167
CLOUD WATCHING

"Do you know how God controls the clouds and makes his lightning flash? Do you know how the clouds hang poised, those wonders of him who has perfect knowledge?"
JOB 37:15–16

God, I'm sitting on the porch, staring out at the horizon, mesmerized by the deep blue sky—like a canvas You're eagerly painting. I imagine You sitting back, then dabbing to create a cloud wisp; with a flourish of Your brush, a rainbow appears.

You offer up sunrises and sunsets and rainbows and rain, and all of this pleases You. God, I love Your creativity. How can I echo this in my day? How can I bring beauty to conversations and work spaces and even my wardrobe? How can I add color and brush moments with kindness? How can I take the peace of cloud watching into my whole day?

God, even in my desire to embrace the beauty You make, please help me so that I don't feel like I have to mimic but simply appreciate Your works. Let me sit in awe of how You design; let me turn my face upward toward the clouds and smile. Amen.

Day 168

SWIMMING IN SUCCESS

Simon Peter said to them, "I am going fishing." The others said, "We will go with you."... That night they caught no fish. Early in the morning Jesus stood on the shore of the lake.... He said to them, "Put your net over the right side of the boat. Then you will catch some fish." They put out the net. They were not able to pull it in because it was so full of fish.... There were 153 big fish.
JOHN 21:3–4, 6, 11 NLV

Jesus, I love this story of how Your discouraged disciples caught no fish. Then You came along, told them what to do, and they ended up catching 153! But the best part was when Peter realized it was You, he jumped into the water and swam to Your side! What an expression of joy!

That's how I feel, Lord. When I'm discouraged, stuck, out of ideas, Your voice comes through. I follow it, and the next thing I know, I'm swimming in success, rushing joyfully to Your side to share my bounty with You! Thank You, Lord, for all the victories You supply, to Your glory. In Jesus' name, I pray, amen.

Day 169
HE'S BIG ENOUGH

Humble yourselves, therefore, under God's mighty hand,
that he may lift you up in due time. Cast all your anxiety on
him because he cares for you. Be alert and of sober mind.
Your enemy the devil prowls around like a roaring lion looking
for someone to devour. Resist him, standing firm in the faith.
1 PETER 5:6–9

Father God, I need a strong shoulder, something sturdy and unmovable to lean on. Without You in my life, I'm consumed with worry, anxiety, and fears. Without You, I'm left with nothing but my own inadequate attempts to cope with my hurts and my uncertainty. Without You, I have no assurance of something greater. But You are here, and You are big enough to handle all my emotions. I can throw my fears onto Your capable shoulders because You care. My consolation stems from the knowledge that You care. A mighty yet unfeeling God would be cold comfort to my anxiety. But I am at peace because You tenderly attend to every detail of Your plan. In the name of Jesus, amen.

Day 170
THE GOOD SHEPHERD'S VOICE

I am the Good Shepherd; and I know and recognize My own, and My own know and recognize Me. . . . The sheep that are My own hear and are listening to My voice; and I know them, and they follow Me. And I give them eternal life, and they shall never lose it or perish throughout the ages. [To all eternity they shall never by any means be destroyed.]
JOHN 10:14, 27–28 AMPC

There was just something about You, Jesus, that attracted me. Perhaps it was Your truth in a world of half truths. Maybe it was the fact that You were both gentle and powerful. Or because You gave Your life for me. But then one day I heard Your Word, Your *voice*—and I was truly and forever hooked. Day after day, hour after hour, I kept coming back to know, hear, and learn more about You and Your ways. To this day, I can't seem to get enough. My beloved Jesus, thank You for shepherding me, giving me eternal life, and giving my soul a craving for Your voice. In Your name I pray. Amen.

Day 171
LOVE REMINDERS

But you, Lord, are a compassionate and gracious God,
slow to anger, abounding in love and faithfulness.
PSALM 86:15

Love is such an ambiguous, big, simple word. Yet, what it contains is the undercurrent of unconditionality. You love unconditionally. You love me when I mess up. You love me when I try but fail. I know this well. I see Your personal reminders in heart shapes in the cream of my coffee. I see leaves scattered underfoot in the shape of hearts. God, I see hearts in makeup splatters, cement designs, and spills.

All these reminders draw me back to love. You are love. You love me. I am loved unconditionally. And even when my soul struggles to understand this, would You please echo this in front of my eyes and bring my heart to scripture and truth so that the constant messaging that I saturate in is love? Deep, simple, unconditional love. In Jesus' name, amen.

Day 172
YOUR PRAYER HAS BEEN HEARD

The angel said to him, "Zacharias, do not be afraid.
Your prayer has been heard. Your wife Elizabeth will give
birth to a son. You are to name him John. You will be glad
and have much joy. Many people will be happy because
he is born. He will be great in the sight of the Lord. . . .
Even from his birth, he will be filled with the Holy Spirit."
LUKE 1:13–15 NLV

I love Your Word, Lord. For it not only gives me a great picture of You, but its stories prove that You are forever working in people's lives. That You *do* answer prayer. That I should never give up praying for something. No matter how many years go by. No matter how old I get. No matter how seemingly impossible my request becomes. I will never lose hope or forget that You hear me when I pray. So here I am, Lord, once more coming to You with the same request. Give me the joy of Your answer, Lord. I await Your reply, praising Your name, knowing my prayer has been heard by the doer of the impossible. Amen.

Day 173
MAGNIFICENT PERFECTION

The heavens proclaim the glory of God. The skies display his craftsmanship. Day after day they continue to speak; night after night they make him known. They speak without a sound or word; their voice is never heard. Yet their message has gone throughout the earth, and their words to all the world. . . . The instructions of the Lord are perfect, reviving the soul.
PSALM 19:1–4, 7 NLT

God of the universe, You are perfection. This world screams Your magnificence and glory at the top of its lungs with the first blush of every morning. All I have to do is listen to the voice of Your creation. The dictionary says that to be perfect is to be flawless and complete, thoroughly skilled or proficient, pure and undiluted. And because perfection is encompassed in Your character, Your guidelines are also perfect. I trust in the utter flawlessness of Your plans and the purity of Your laws, for they can be nothing less, since to be lacking anything would contradict Your perfection. My hope is bolstered by the knowledge that I serve a God incapable of making a mistake. In Jesus' name, amen.

Day 174
CONTINUAL BLESSING

I will bless the Lord at all times; His praise shall continually
be in my mouth. My life makes its boast in the Lord;
let the humble and afflicted hear and be glad. O magnify
the Lord with me, and let us exalt His name together.
I sought (inquired of) the Lord and required Him [of
necessity and on the authority of His Word], and He
heard me, and delivered me from all my fears.
PSALM 34:1–4 AMPC

No matter what is happening in my life, in my world, it is You, God, that I bless. For You hear me when I pray. Your love and kindness, Your compassion and mercy are all-encompassing. You make my life worth living. Life is no life at all when I'm tied up in troubles, distressed by doubts, and frantic with fears. So I come to You. When I enter Your presence, Your light obliterates my problems, indecisiveness, and insecurities. They fade into nothingness. And all that remains are Your light, warmth, and love. This is why I seek You, serve You, celebrate You, and surrender to You. In Jesus' name, amen.

Day 175
STAYING IN PEACE

Let the peace of Christ rule in your hearts, since as members of one body you were called to peace. And be thankful.
COLOSSIANS 3:15

Lord, I find myself wanting to stay in this sanctuary space of peace where You dwell and simultaneously wanting to burst through and take action. I want to make things happen and kick into old habits and say, "Look at me. Look at what I'm doing. Aren't I amazing and talented?" I'm sorry. I'm sorry I want to be seen by the world. And yet I know that leaving this space of peace isn't worth it because it forces me to do life on my own instead of accepting the fact that Your peace is a gift that I can settle into.

God, I ask for Your strength when I'm tempted to leave this space of peace because of discomfort. May this discomfort be a bed of comfort. May I know You are near even as I hold the tension of wanting to leave this space and wanting to stay here forever. Help me find the balance, please. Amen.

Day 176
TREES OF THE WOODS

"The Lord made the heavens. Honor and great power are with Him. Strength and joy are in His place. . . . Let the heavens be glad. Let the earth be filled with joy. And let them say among the nations, 'The Lord rules!' Let the sea thunder, and all that is in it. Let the field be happy, and all that is in it. Then the trees of the woods will sing for joy before the Lord."
1 CHRONICLES 16:26–27, 31–33 NLV

What joy I find in the idea, in the fact that *You* are the Grand Creator, Lord. All I see—and all I do not see—has been made by Your hands. You are so great, powerful, and wonderful. All the strength and joy are where You are, and You are everywhere—even inside me as I abide in You. So I am rejoicing in that today, Lord. I trust in You, knowing You are in charge, controlling all things—places, people, and events! What a wonderful world You've created, one in which even the trees sing for joy before You! Be with me in this moment, Lord, as I take a nature walk and bask in the joy of Your making. Amen.

Day 177

FOREVER THE SAME

Remember your leaders, who spoke the word of God to you. Consider the outcome of their way of life and imitate their faith. Jesus Christ is the same yesterday and today and forever. Do not be carried away by all kinds of strange teachings. It is good for our hearts to be strengthened by grace, not by eating ceremonial foods, which is of no benefit to those who do so.
HEBREWS 13:7–9

Father, the fads of this world change faster than I can adapt—clothing trends shift from wide-legged pants to skinny jeans; numerous diets come and go, from Atkins to South Beach to Whole 30. . .who can keep up? But in a world that's swirling in change, there is a constant as old as eternity. You, Lord, do not shift. You're comfortingly always the same as You were yesterday. And You'll still be the same tomorrow as You are today. Your Word does not alter. I can hold any "trendy" new belief against the ageless pillar of scripture and determine its truth. Your unshifting character brings hope to my faith because Your promises of old will forever be upheld. In Jesus' name, amen.

Day 178

A WAY OF WORSHIP

Listen to me; I will teach you to revere and worshipfully fear the Lord. What man is he who desires life and longs for many days, that he may see good? Keep your tongue from evil and your lips from speaking deceit. Depart from evil and do good; seek, inquire for, and crave peace and pursue (go after) it! The eyes of the Lord are toward the [uncompromisingly] righteous and His ears are open to their cry.
PSALM 34:11–15 AMPC

These days, Lord, so many people are hurting others because they're no longer careful with words, whether those words are spoken, texted, tweeted, emailed, snail-mailed, or quoted. But words do have power. So, as I continue on my peace trail, I'm going to follow Your direction to watch what I say. To make sure my words are not just true but encouraging. To leave evil behind and make it a point to do good each day. And most of all, Lord, I'm going to make it my aim and passion not just to rest in peace but to look for, crave, and pursue it. That will be my way of worshipping You here on earth and in heaven above. Amen.

Day 179
UNCOMFORTABLE PEOPLE

*"Why do you see the speck that is in your brother's eye,
but do not notice the log that is in your own eye? Or how
can you say to your brother, 'Let me take the speck out
of your eye,' when there is the log in your own eye?"*
MATTHEW 7:3–4 ESV

God, I'm thankful that, although I'm uncomfortable, You put people in my path who are different than I am so I can learn a different facet of who You are. If the image of You is in everybody (and it is), then I get to meet different facets of Your essence and Your perspective through others.

Forgive me for being quick to categorize or to assume I won't be friends with someone if there isn't an instant connection. Is there a part of my personality that needs to be softened by being around this person? Am I willing to do life and journey with those who are uncomfortable for me? In this discomfort, please help me find that the connection piece is You. You love all Your people the same, and there is beauty in learning from those who, with only one look, I may miss out on knowing. In Jesus' name, amen.

Day 180

BLESSED BELIEF

*[Elizabeth] cried out. . . . Blessed (happy, to be envied)
is she who believed that there would be a fulfillment of
the things that were spoken to her from the Lord. And
Mary said, My soul magnifies and extols the Lord, and my
spirit rejoices in God my Savior, for He has looked upon
the low station and humiliation of His handmaiden. . . .
For He Who is almighty has done great things for me.*
LUKE 1:42, 45–49 AMPC

I find my strength and joy, Lord, when I believe that You will do
what Your Word says, when I have faith that You will keep Your
promises to those who love You. Help me build up that belief
and faith, Lord, more and more each day. Remind me each and
every moment that through Your Word, strength, and power,
I will find my way through this life, and my soul and spirit will
rejoice over You in good times and not-so-good times. Help me
base my life on the fact that You are doing great things for me
and in me. In Jesus' name and power, I pray, amen.

Day 181

UNIMAGINABLY MORE

*Now to him who is able to do immeasurably more than all
we ask or imagine, according to his power that is at work
within us, to him be glory in the church and in Christ Jesus
throughout all generations, for ever and ever! Amen.*
EPHESIANS 3:20–21

Lord, praying to You is easier than calling a friend for a chat. In
the midst of this accessibility, sometimes I forget how amazing
it is that I can pray to the living God. You will listen to me! And
You're not just a sympathetic ear. Your Word says that You have
the power to do immeasurably more than all I ask or imagine.
Help me to pray expectantly and passionately and continually
to the only one who can really change things. Your fantastic
power is working within me. Keep working on me until I become
the daughter You desire. And when my answers don't seem to
be exactly what I'd hoped for, help me remember that You
imagine more and think bigger than I do. Amen.

Day 182

CATCHING YOUR BREATH

Is anyone crying for help? God is listening, ready to rescue you. If your heart is broken, you'll find God right there; if you're kicked in the gut, he'll help you catch your breath. Disciples so often get into trouble; still, God is there every time.
PSALM 34:17–19 MSG

Spirit of the Lord, troubles seem to be everywhere! Each day it seems harder and harder to maintain any kind of peace. Yet that's what You bring. But You cannot bring it if I don't cry out for it. So help me to be more willing to come to You and share my troubles. Help me to be humble enough to ask for and accept whatever help You can bring me. I cannot live this life on my own. Too often I need an advocate—one who can translate my thoughts, remove the stains on my heart, and relieve the weight on my soul. Come close, hold me tight, and heal this broken heart. Help me catch my breath. Be here every time. Bring Your peace, Your protection, Your love, Your healing, Your power, and Your strength. Amen.

Day 183

LIVING AWAKE

For anything that becomes visible is light.
Therefore it says, "Awake, O sleeper, and arise
from the dead, and Christ will shine on you."
EPHESIANS 5:14 ESV

At church we read a prayer, and a few words connected to my soul: *open, empty, awake.* God, please help me live awake every day. Help me look for You in the details and people.

Where do You want me to live fully, with eyes open, palms out, and a heart surrendered to where Your Spirit is guiding and moving? God, where are You inviting me to live awake? Where am I sleepy or shut down?

God, I'm asking Your Spirit to gently pull back the covers and help me to my feet so that I may live awake. For when I live awake in Your Spirit, I live alive. And this is where You are glorified. So I ask: Where is Your attentive gaze drawing me to live awake? What does this look like today? In Jesus' name, amen.

Day 184
THE WAY TO WISDOM

Happy is the man who finds wisdom, and the man who gets understanding. . . . She is worth more than stones of great worth. Nothing you can wish for compares with her. Long life is in her right hand. Riches and honor are in her left hand. Her ways are pleasing, and all her paths are peace. . . . Happy are all who hold her near.
PROVERBS 3:13, 15–18 NLV

I want to search out Your knowledge, Lord, to understand what You want me to do, say, and think. Show me the path toward Your wisdom. May I pray for that more than anything else. That is where I will find my direction. That is where I will find the answers I need. That is where I will discover the way You want me to go. So guide my reading of Your Word today, Lord. Show me what You want me to read. Tell me what You'd have me memorize and write upon my heart. Equip me with all I need to know so I can best serve You and find joy along the way. In Jesus' name, I pray, amen.

Day 185
A SENSE OF PEACE

*May all go well with those who are right and good.
And may there be much peace until the moon is no
more. . . . For He will take out of trouble the one in need
when he cries for help, and the poor man who has no one
to help. He will have loving-pity on the weak and those
in need. He will save the lives of those in need. He will
take them from the bad power that is held over them.*
PSALM 72:7, 12–14 NLV

To know that someday justice will be served, that at some point
people will be helped and avenged, gives me a sense of peace
today. In the meantime, Lord, help me do what I can to alleviate
pain and increase the right and good in the lives of people who
have no one to help. Use me as Your instrument to do what I
can for the helpless in the moment and leave what I cannot do
to You. Show me today where You would have me help the helpless and give aid and offer prayers for those who need them. In
Jesus' name, amen.

Day 186
WELL AND WHOLE

*I call to God; GOD will help me. At dusk, dawn, and noon
I sigh deep sighs—he hears, he rescues. My life is well
and whole, secure in the middle of danger. . . . Pile your
troubles on GOD's shoulders—he'll carry your load, he'll
help you out. He'll never let good people topple into ruin.*
PSALM 55:16–18, 22 MSG

Lord, right now in this moment "my insides are turned inside
out; specters of death have me down. I shake with fear, I shud-
der from head to foot. 'Who will give me wings,' I ask—'wings
like a dove?' Get me out of here on dove wings; I want some
peace and quiet. I want a walk in the country, I want a cabin in
the woods. I'm desperate for a change from rage and stormy
weather" (Psalm 55:4–8 MSG). So, Lord, I'm calling on You, certain You'll help me, hear me, and rescue me. I know that even
though I may find myself in the middle of danger, I'm safe and
secure within You. When I find You, my troubles slide off my
shoulders and onto Yours. I know You, God, are strong and can
carry my load. For this I thank You. Amen.

Day 187

GROWTH

But grow in the grace and knowledge of our Lord and Savior Jesus Christ. To him be the glory both now and to the day of eternity. Amen.
2 PETER 3:18 ESV

God, I notice that in order to grow, I have to put down something to pick up something new. With this comes grief. I grieve what no longer fits, what I'm outgrowing. Lord, would You please continue speaking to me about what needs to die so that my spirit can hold the new work You are doing?

What coping mechanisms, habits, or comforts are You inviting me to put down? Where are You inviting me into a new way of living? I apologize for beating myself up for feeling embarrassed for grieving what has died. I know this is necessary to heal, and I ask for healing and comfort where growth means death in some way.

I want to continue walking into hope. Hope is life. I don't want to neglect what I'm leaving behind, but to celebrate that it was beautiful for a season. Please remind me where I need to grieve what's been outgrown and step forward into growth. In Jesus' name, amen.

Day 188

STARSTRUCK

The star [the wise men] had seen in the East went before them. It came and stopped over the place where the young Child was. When they saw the star, they were filled with much joy. They went into the house and found the young Child with Mary, His mother. Then they got down before Him and worshiped Him. They opened their bags of riches and gave Him gifts. . . . Then God spoke to them.
MATTHEW 2:9–12 NLV

Jesus, I, like the wise men, followed the light and found You. What joy I discovered in You at our first meeting! What a journey it has been. What wonder I experience each day when I get down on my knees and worship You. I offer You my life, heart, body, mind, and soul. Yet if there are other gifts You would like me to hand over to You or share with others, please show me what they are. For my journey with You has just begun. I want to be Your hands and feet, serving You until I am with You on the other side. Speak to me, Lord. Show me the way to grow ever closer to You. In Your name, I pray, amen.

Day 189

CLEAR THE WAY

*Night and day we pray most earnestly that we may
see you again and supply what is lacking in your
faith. Now may our God and Father himself and our
Lord Jesus clear the way for us to come to you.*
1 THESSALONIANS 3:10–11

God, I don't see a way forward through all the problems assaulting me. Everything I attempt ends in utter failure. How am I to move forward? Show me the way, because You are the great way maker. You can bust down the walls in my path. You can remove the obstacles that hinder my journey. When all seems hopeless, You alone can clear the way. You have the power to open avenues I never imagined possible. Supply what is lacking in my faith and trust. I'm waiting expectantly for You to make a game-changing move. I will ask continually until I see the path You have prepared for me. In the powerful name of Jesus, amen.

Day 190

MIND LIFE AND SOUL PEACE

Those who are according to the flesh and are controlled
by its unholy desires set their minds on and pursue
those things which gratify the flesh, but those who are
according to the Spirit and are controlled by the desires
of the Spirit set their minds on and seek those things which
gratify the [Holy] Spirit. Now the mind of the flesh [which is
sense and reason without the Holy Spirit] is death. . . .
But the mind of the [Holy] Spirit is life and [soul] peace.
ROMANS 8:5–6 AMPC

Too often, Lord, I find myself being controlled by unhealthy desires, ones that have me looking to gratify bodily yearnings above all else. But living that kind of life gives me no sense of real peace at all. So I need and want to change things up, to have my mind controlled by the desires of the Spirit. To set my mind on seeking things that will please the Spirit. For then and only then will I find peace for both my mind *and* my soul. Amen.

Day 191

WHEN I'M TEMPTED TO OVEREXTEND MYSELF

He says, "Be still, and know that I am God; I will be exalted among the nations, I will be exalted in the earth."
PSALM 46:10

Lord, I realize that sometimes I don't have to overextend myself. I can sit back and just be. There's so much comfort and grace in not having to be untrue to myself to be loved or to perform to get applause or to talk to be noticed.

I can cozy up and just listen. I can listen to You and to people around me. I can listen to Your Spirit in me. I confess that I notice how often I feel the need to overextend and give more than necessary. So, God, I ask for Your permission and Your gentle grace to guide me as I listen. I long to experience that deep knowing that occurs as I settle into how You tether my soul and weight me with grace. I can sit and just be and know that I'm okay. I'm okay. I'm okay. And perhaps being okay is the biggest grace today. In Jesus' name, amen.

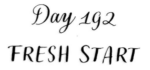

Day 192
FRESH START

Count yourself lucky, how happy you must be—you get a fresh start, your slate's wiped clean. Count yourself lucky—God holds nothing against you and you're holding nothing back from him. When I kept it all inside, my bones turned to powder, my words became daylong groans. . . . Then I let it all out; I said, "I'll come clean about my failures to God." Suddenly the pressure was gone—my guilt dissolved, my sin disappeared.
PSALM 32:1–3, 5 MSG

Lord, when I keep things from You, when I don't admit to You (or myself) that I've done something wrong, it eats me up inside. One wrongdoing piles up onto another and another, and before I know it, I feel like I'm about to implode. So here I am today, Lord, telling You not just the good things I've done but the not-so-good. And I ask Your forgiveness in the process. For then I will once again be able to tap into joy, happy in God, counting myself lucky in the Lord, who not only removes my sin and guilt but makes them disappear—forever! What a relief! In Jesus' name, amen.

Day 193
RADIANT

*I sought the LORD, and he answered me; he delivered
me from all my fears. Those who look to him are
radiant; their faces are never covered with shame.*

PSALM 34:4–5

Father, I have felt shame. I have done things that I don't want anyone to see. I wish I could hide them and never think of them again. Their stain taints my life. I kick my thoughts of them to the dark corners, but You already know all about everything I've ever done, every misstep, every sin, every regret. And yet You still want me! You've forgiven me. You answered when I went looking for You, and You've delivered me from shame and replaced my sorrow with radiance. Instead of outcast and rejection, You've given me a new name. You've called me precious daughter, the apple of Your eye. I no longer feel ashamed. I'm glowing with Your love and approval. In Jesus' name, amen.

Day 194
POWER DOWN

People at the top. . .have it made. . .have nothing to worry about, not a care in the whole wide world. . . . Pretentious with arrogance, they wear the latest fashions in violence, pampered and overfed, decked out in silk bows of silliness. They jeer, using words to kill; they bully their way with words. They're full of hot air, loudmouths disturbing the peace. People actually listen to them—can you believe it? Like thirsty puppies, they lap up their words.
PSALM 73:3–10 MSG

When I was younger, Lord, it seemed that people had more respect for each other and for the truth. But these days, those things seem not to matter. And the only thing that does matter is money—who has it and who doesn't have it. But that's not going to matter in my life. I'm no longer going to worry about the "people at the top," those who seem to have it all. But I am going to ask You, Lord, to power down bullies in this town, county, state, and country. From all walks of life, all families, all jobs, and all people in government and beyond. Help me, Lord, to better discern peace breakers and spend more time with the peacemakers. In Jesus' name, amen.

Day 195

SURRENDERING THE IDEAL

"Can you fathom the mysteries of God? Can you probe the limits of the Almighty? They are higher than the heavens above—what can you do? They are deeper than the depths below—what can you know? Their measure is longer than the earth and wider than the sea."

JOB 11:7–9

God, I confess I live for the ideal. The what-can-be. The best-case scenario. And with this longing for ideal, I find myself disappointed. Disappointed at what is. And disappointed at what could be. Because *all of life* can be so beautiful. Yet, You are making beauty even in the hard. Even in the confusion and not-as-it-should-be, You are breaking through and saying, "I Am."

Forgive me, Lord, for idolizing the ideal more than the reality of knowing You. Knowing You is enough because where You are is ideal. You are in the broken relationships and darkness. You are in the suffering and pain. You are in the not-just-yet. But deeper still is the beauty that You created me with a longing for more. And may this more be You. Kind, loving, omnipotent, mysterious *You*.

Lord, lift my face to see Yours and behold Your beauty. Your beauty beckons me onward and upward. Amen.

Day 196
THE GETAWAY

"Are you tired? Worn out? Burned out on religion? Come to me. Get away with me and you'll recover your life. I'll show you how to take a real rest. Walk with me and work with me—watch how I do it. Learn the unforced rhythms of grace. I won't lay anything heavy or ill-fitting on you. Keep company with me and you'll learn to live freely and lightly."
MATTHEW 11:28–30 MSG

Lord Jesus, joy is elusive at best when I'm not getting the rest I need—spiritually, mentally, emotionally, and physically. I'm worn out, burned out, and just plain tired. Exhausted. So I'm not just coming to You but limping to You. Please take this load of cares, worries, and woes off my back. Help me to give them up, to lay them at Your feet. Show me how to really rest. Teach me how to keep pace with and work with You. Help me walk in the "unforced rhythms of grace." Teach me how to live this life freely yet more fully. To bear Your light load so I may once more find joy. In Your name, amen.

Day 197

CHOSEN TO LOVE

"A servant does not know his master's business. Instead, I have called you friends, for everything that I learned from my Father I have made known to you. You did not choose me, but I chose you and appointed you so that you might go and bear fruit—fruit that will last—and so that whatever you ask in my name the Father will give you. This is my command: Love each other."
JOHN 15:15–17

Father, too often I haven't chosen You with my actions. Instead I've betrayed You, as Judas did. I've sold You out for the glittering silver of my own desires, my comfort, my glory, and my own self-seeking gain. But that isn't the end of the story. Yes, Judas betrayed You with a kiss, but You still chose him, even when You knew his love for You wouldn't be true. And You've chosen me as well, not because I chose You but because You love me. You appointed me to bear lasting fruit. You called me friend instead of enemy. Lord, help me to choose You back—to choose to love others instead of self. In Jesus' name, amen.

Day 198
WHEN ALL'S RIGHT

Right will build a home in the fertile field. And where there's Right, there'll be Peace and the progeny of Right: quiet lives and endless trust. My people will live in a peaceful neighborhood—in safe houses, in quiet gardens. The forest of your pride will be clear-cut, the city showing off your power leveled. But you will enjoy a fortunate life, planting well-watered fields and gardens, with your farm animals grazing freely.
ISAIAH 32:16–20 MSG

There are days, Lord, when I despair of finding the peace I crave within and without. And then I enter the land of Your words, which soothe my soul and buoy my spirit. For You speak of how when all is right, we will find peace. And in that place of right and peace, I'll find the quiet life and endless trust I yearn for, surrounded by peace, safety, and calmness. Clear away my pride as if it were flammable brush. I know that I can only get to that place of peace with the help of Your words and Your powerful Spirit. Take me there now, Lord. Show me the freedom of a quiet life and endless trust. In Jesus' name, amen.

Day 199

REST IN THE RUSH

Then, because so many people were coming and going that they did not even have a chance to eat, he said to them, "Come with me by yourselves to a quiet place and get some rest."

MARK 6:31

My soul feels rushed. There's no need to rush except for the deadline I put on myself. Why do I feel rushed?

Lord, I need Your calm today. I confess that I sense anxiety pulling at me, and more than ever, I need Your rest. Your deep, settled soul rest that anchors and pulls me back to Your throne room. This sanctuary space I often feel tempted to leave is exactly where You are calling. There's a tension here. A tension to stay with You and launch myself into the sea of rush. Deep breath in. Deep breath out.

Calm my mind, Lord. Still my soul. Weight me with Your love. Lord, please forgive me for living without margin and caving to a frantic pace. Oh, how I need Your rest today. Where Your rest is offered, help me find my way to You. Amen.

Day 200

GROUNDED IN THE WORD

"The seed which fell between rocks is like the person who receives the Word with joy as soon as he hears it. Its root is not deep and it does not last long. When troubles and suffering come because of the Word, he gives up and falls away. . . . The seed which fell on good ground is like the one who hears the Word and understands it. He gives much grain."
MATTHEW 13:20–21, 23 NLV

I am so glad, Lord, that, at first hearing, I not only took in Your Word with joy but let it take root deep within me. But now sometimes on especially busy days, I find myself not making digging into Your Word a priority. Help me to change that, Lord. To look to You and Your Word before my day begins, before my feet hit the floor. Help me to go deeper and deeper into what You have to say. And help me grow in my prayer life. For I want to be one of Your good and faithful servants. I want to be so fruitful that I please You more than anyone or anything else, including myself. Amen.

Day 201
CLEANSED

Don't you realize that this is not the way to live? Unjust people who don't care about God will not be joining in his kingdom. Those who use and abuse each other, use and abuse sex, use and abuse the earth and everything in it, don't qualify as citizens in God's kingdom. A number of you know from experience what I'm talking about, for not so long ago you were on that list. Since then, you've been cleaned up and given a fresh start by Jesus, our Master, our Messiah, and by our God present in us, the Spirit.

1 CORINTHIANS 6:9–11 MSG

Father in heaven, I feel the filth of my sin. I am well acquainted with the shame that comes with being considered dirty and unworthy. I've knowingly done things that are wrong in Your eyes. But You have plunged me into a clear spring of water. Your Son's blood has scoured away all of my sin until I'm sparkling and pristine before You. I no longer need to hide my ratty rags in the darkness. Instead I step into the light and come closer to You, assured by my faith in You that I have been washed and purified. You no longer see my past. Instead You see me draped in robes of holiness. My conscience is clean! In Jesus' name, amen.

Day 202
HOPE AND HARMONY

Whatever was written in the past was written for our instruction, so that we may have hope through endurance and through the encouragement from the Scriptures. Now may the God who gives endurance and encouragement allow you to live in harmony with one another, according to the command of Christ Jesus. . . . Now may the God of hope fill you with all joy and peace as you believe in Him so that you may overflow with hope by the power of the Holy Spirit.
ROMANS 15:4–5, 13 HCSB

Your scriptures, Lord, are my gateway to You. Your stories help me understand who You are and how I can grow closer and closer to You. Your testaments encourage me to learn more about who You are and how You see me. Your psalms read like my journal, where a myriad of emotions and thoughts align so well with my own. Your Word makes me feel loved, whole, and full of hope. God of fortitude and confidence, help me find a way to live in peace with others, just as Christ commanded I do. Spirit of hope, fill me with Your joy and peace. Amen.

Day 203
DELIGHTING IN DIFFERENCES

*There is neither Jew nor Greek, there is neither
slave nor free, there is no male and female,
for you are all one in Christ Jesus.*
GALATIANS 3:28 ESV

Differences can divide. Differences in politics and person-
alities and church preferences. Differences are where the
enemy wreaks havoc and tears relationships, families, and
churches apart.

Lord, where am I allowing differences to divide? Where am I
focusing on what polarizes instead of what connects and heals?
Please lovingly convict me in this area, and invite me to notice
how You are bridging all of humanity to You. In my prayer, God,
illuminate differences as an invitation to learn from others, to
ask about their perspective, to be open to new ways of seeing
and believing.

Where am I rigid and hard? Where am I judgmental and critical? Where am I pretentious and right? Soften me, Lord.

As I soften, may these different viewpoints melt into a kalei-
doscope of humanity—unique ways Your Spirit moves through
every race, language, doctrine, and opinion. Be my bridge, Father. Connect me to Your mercy and make me into a soft, mold-
able soul. In Jesus' name, amen.

Day 204
A HIDING PLACE

*Let all who are God-like pray to You while You may
be found, because in the floods of much water, they
will not touch him. You are my hiding place. You keep
me safe from trouble. . . . Many are the sorrows of
the sinful. But loving-kindness will be all around
the man who trusts in the Lord. Be glad in the Lord
and be full of joy, you who are right with God!*
PSALM 32:6–7, 10–11 NLV

I am always amazed, Lord, at how You keep me out of troubles seen and unseen. With You next to me, above me, below me, behind me, before me, and within me, I find I am truly safe no matter what comes my way. You, Lord, are my hiding place. To You I run. In You I trust. Surround me not only with Your power, strength, and presence but with all Your unfathomable loving-kindness as I praise You and pray to You. Keep my feet upon Your good path. And in You I will find not only joy but everything I need. In Jesus' name, amen.

Day 205

HIS STORY OF HOPE

For everything that was written in the past was
written to teach us, so that through the endurance
taught in the Scriptures and the encouragement
they provide we might have hope.

ROMANS 15:4

God, just when it looks like the good guys are poised on the brink of failure, my favorite superhero charges onto the screen. Who doesn't love a good fantasy? They encourage us to strive for more in our own lives—more courage, more honor, more strength. It's fun to imagine new worlds, even though, in the end, they're not real. But the Bible is not just another collection of fairy tales. Every word of scripture is true and effective for teaching and encouragement. Thank You for writing down Your great story of the ages! You knew without it we would slip into despair. So You penned Your love and Your plans for us to spur us by hope toward endurance. In Jesus' name, amen.

Day 206
BEHIND GOD'S BACK

This is the writing of Hezekiah king of Judah after he had been sick and had recovered from his sickness. . . . O give me back my health and make me live! Behold, it was for my peace that I had intense bitterness; but You have loved back my life from the pit of corruption and nothingness, for You have cast all my sins behind Your back.
ISAIAH 38:9, 16–17 AMPC

Sometimes, Lord, it's the bitterness of our lives that leads us to seek You, to find You, to pray to You and ask You things we would otherwise remain silent about. Our needs, our desires, our predicaments draw us to You time and time again. And time and time again, during and after we pray to You, Lord, we find ourselves overwhelmed by the power of Your peace and Your love. For only You, Lord, could love us back away from the edge of the cliff. Only You can grant the mercy and forgiveness we need. Only You can be and are our God. In Jesus' name, amen.

Day 207
MORE MANNA

"And he humbled you and let you hunger and fed you with manna, which you did not know, nor did your fathers know, that he might make you know that man does not live by bread alone, but man lives by every word that comes from the mouth of the Lord."
DEUTERONOMY 8:3 ESV

God, in the Old Testament, You offered manna to the Israelites. Enough for that day. Miraculous morning nourishment. God, I want Your manna as well. More of You. More everyday miracles and soul nourishment and daily reminders that You are providing and showing up and feeding my soul, mind, and body.

Where are You offering manna? Where are You providing and gifting and sending miracle reminders? Where am I neglecting to look down and find Your ground-covering gift? Lead me to Your manna, Lord. Let me nourish on Your truth. I long to fill myself with a content spirit and speak of the wondrous ways You cut through real time and provide.

Manna. Bring this word to my lips, and may I echo it throughout the day. *More manna.* More life. More miracles. More You. Thank You, Lord, for how You are providing. Amen.

Day 208
GOD—GIVEN JOY

There is nothing better for a man than to eat and drink and find joy in his work. I have seen that this also is from the hand of God. For who can. . .find joy without Him? For God has given wisdom and much learning and joy to the person who is good in God's eyes. But to the sinner He has given the work of. . .getting many riches together to give to the one who pleases God.
ECCLESIASTES 2:24–26 NLV

Lord, some days I find myself not enjoying anything. But now I realize that's because my thoughts and focus are not on You. For only when I seek You first and bring You to mind throughout my day do I find the joy I crave. So remind me of Your presence, Lord, as I eat and drink. And especially as I work. For I'm not really working for my boss, my family, my church, my spouse, or my school. No, I'm working for You. You are my source of true joy. All I do, I do for You alone. For that work, those duties are what truly last forever and ever. I pray and praise in Jesus' name, amen.

Day 209
NO GIMMICKS

"Peace I leave with you; my peace I give you. I do not give to you as the world gives. Do not let your hearts be troubled and do not be afraid."
JOHN 14:27

Lord, if something looks too good to be true, we know that it usually is. Why? Because in this fallen world, it seems that everyone, no matter how altruistic their actions appear, has ulterior motives or a self-serving angle. Is anyone truly selfless and good? Only You. The hidden strings of this world are absent from Your gifts. You give out of pure, unadulterated love. Your gifts are real, not an illusion. Your peace is legitimate and substantial. It won't break down two hours after the warranty expires. It's truly unlimited coverage, and it permeates every facet of my life, coating me in the calm of Your love. Lord, make me a genuine article in Your likeness. Let me give freely, expecting nothing. In Jesus' name, amen.

Day 210
SO MUCH

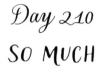

The Lord Who bought you and saves you, the Holy One of Israel, says, "I am the Lord your God, Who teaches you to do well, Who leads you in the way you should go. If only you had listened to My Laws! Then your peace would have been like a river and your right-standing with God would have been like the waves of the sea."
ISAIAH 48:17–18 NLV

Ah Lord, there is so much I owe You, so much You've done for me that I can never repay. Yet there are some things I *can* do to honor You. I can abide by Your teachings, so please make Your lessons plain, Lord. I can follow Your leading, so open my eyes to Your signposts. And I can listen to Your Word; open my ears so I can clearly hear You. Then I will have Your perpetual and constantly flowing peace. Then I will find Your blessings coming to me like waves rolling in from the sea. Ah Lord, there is so much I owe You, forever and ever. Amen.

Day 211

AWARENESS OF WHO OR WHAT TO FORGIVE

Examine yourselves, to see whether you are in the faith. Test yourselves. Or do you not realize this about yourselves, that Jesus Christ is in you?—unless indeed you fail to meet the test!
2 Corinthians 13:5 esv

Lord, as I seek Your strength to forgive, I admit I'm not sure what or who I ought to forgive. I ask for awareness. What are small, physical ways that my body hints at resentment or anger? Where do I bristle inside? Who do I find myself uncomfortable or frustrated with? Why? Where do I have trouble giving love and patience and an objective response?

I ask for Your awareness, Lord. For in paying attention, Your Spirit is shining tiny lights on where forgiveness is lacking. And how am I to forgive if I'm unaware of the sources?

In my prayer for awareness, please protect me, Jesus. Keep the enemy far from my ears and heart, and keep my tendency to blame at bay. May I walk into every moment with eyes open and my heart aware of what I am feeling, sensing, and thinking. I trust You to journey with me in my awareness and draw me toward healing and wholeness. In Jesus' name, amen.

Day 212
GIVING CHEERFULLY

He who sows sparingly will also reap sparingly, and he who sows bountifully will also reap bountifully. So let each one give as he purposes in his heart, not grudgingly or of necessity; for God loves a cheerful giver. And God is able to make all grace abound toward you, that you, always having all sufficiency in all things, may have an abundance for every good work.
2 Corinthians 9:6–8 nkjv

When things are difficult financially, Lord, it's hard to give with a cheerful heart. But then I remember Your law: those who give little will get little, but those who give much will get much. So help me keep that in mind, knowing that when I give cheerfully, no matter what my circumstances, I will reap cheerfully, beginning with a bountiful crop of joy. And I will also reap contentment. For as I give, You promise to supply me with everything I might need for all the work I'm doing in and for You. Ah, what a relief to live with the knowledge that as I bless others, I can count on You blessing me. Thank You, God, for all this and so much more. Amen.

Day 213
GOD'S LONGING

Yet the LORD longs to be gracious to you; therefore he
will rise up to show you compassion. For the LORD is a
God of justice. Blessed are all who wait for him!
ISAIAH 30:18

God, I don't need creamy chocolate ice cream sprinkled with delicious bits of chewy chocolate truffle—and maybe drizzled with fudge. It's not essential to my nutrition, and I'm certainly not starving. But did I mention it was chocolate? I just really, really want it. It's amazing to me that You, the God of everything, want to be with me and long to be gracious to me. Even when I betray You, Your love for me remains faithful and true. The depth of Your compassion is unfathomable to me. I'm unworthy of Your grace, and yet Your desire for me to have it surpasses even my mammoth chocolate cravings. Prepare my heart with repentance so I can walk in Your grace. In the name of Jesus, amen.

Day 214
IN GOOD HANDS

The fruit of the [Holy] Spirit [the work which His presence within accomplishes] is love, joy (gladness), peace, patience (an even temper, forbearance), kindness, goodness (benevolence), faithfulness, gentleness (meekness, humility), self-control (self-restraint, continence). . . . If we live by the [Holy] Spirit, let us also walk by the Spirit. [If by the Holy Spirit we have our life in God, let us go forward walking in line, our conduct controlled by the Spirit.]
GALATIANS 5:22–23, 25 AMPC

Lord, You have created me, Your Son has saved me, and Your Spirit produces in me all the positive characteristics—love, joy, peace, patience, kindness, goodness, faithfulness, gentleness, self-control—of a godly daughter. Help me, Lord, to allow Your Spirit to work in me in every and any way He can. Make me look, speak, act, listen, and walk just as Jesus did. I wish to follow in His steps, even though at times I know that road may be rocky. Still, no matter what the terrain, I know I am in good hands, moving forward, my steps solidly in line with Yours and my actions controlled by Your Spirit. Amen.

Day 215
WHEN I'M CONFUSED

So do not throw away your confidence; it will be richly rewarded. You need to persevere so that when you have done the will of God, you will receive what he has promised.
HEBREWS 10:35–36

God, sometimes I don't understand Your ways. You say "be still" in order to know that You are God, but the world tells me, "Work hard. Put yourself out there. Take action."

I feel the tension and wonder, *Which one is it? Do I stay still, or do I strive? Do I put myself out there?* I confess to You that I feel confused with this tension. I feel angry. I am frustrated with You asking me to sit and listen and notice and pay attention to where You are working, and yet simultaneously I wonder, *How will anything happen while I'm just "be"ing?*

So I bring this confusion to You and confess that I don't know what to do with it. Yet, I trust that You are doing a beautiful transformative work in asking me to "be." Perhaps this is the tension of trust? Belief that You are doing something even though I cannot see it? I trust You are doing something in the confusing, unseen pockets. In Jesus' name, amen.

Day 216
GRAND PLANS

Sing for joy in the Lord, you who are right with Him. . . . For the Word of the Lord is right. He is faithful in all He does. . . . Honor Him. For He spoke, and it was done. He spoke with strong words, and it stood strong. . . . The plans of the Lord stand forever. . . . Happy are the people He has chosen for His own.
PSALM 33:1, 4, 8–9, 11–12 NLV

Your Word is amazing, Father God. Your plans never fail. Your promises are sure and certain. You speak and it is done. You said, "Let there be light," and there was light. Help me, Lord, to trust both You and Your Word. To do as You would have me do. Help me not to be discouraged when things don't go the way I planned. Remind me that *You* are the master planner and that *I can trust* in Your plans. As I abide by Your Word, continually strengthened, guided, and empowered, I find the joy You have waiting for me. For I, Your chosen daughter, rest upon Your promises. Thank You, Father God. Amen.

Day 217
SECOND CHANCES

"I now establish my covenant with you and with your descendants after you and with every living creature that was with you—the birds, the livestock and all the wild animals, all those that came out of the ark with you—every living creature on earth. I establish my covenant with you: Never again will all life be destroyed by the waters of a flood; never again will there be a flood to destroy the earth."

Genesis 9:9–11

God, You didn't have to give us another chance. Your beautiful creation had been corrupted. Wickedness and evil were stomping the life out of goodness and love in the hearts of Your masterpiece. How that must have grieved You, just as it pierces a mother to see her children hurting one another. You could have ended it all that day, swept away the brokenness with the decisive hand of a tsunami. But You didn't. Instead You saved a family to begin again. And You made us a promise. But Your love was too great to stop there. Because You are a God of mercy and love, You sent us Your Son to repair the breach in our relationship once and for all—You sent us salvation. Amen.

Day 218
THE REAL THING

*While there has never been any question about your honesty
in these matters—I couldn't be more proud of you!—I want
you also to be smart, making sure every "good" thing
is the real thing. Don't be gullible in regard to smooth-
talking evil. Stay alert like this, and before you know it
the God of peace will come down on Satan with both feet,
stomping him into the dirt. Enjoy the best of Jesus!*
ROMANS 16:19–20 MSG

There are times, Lord, when I feel so gullible, so naive. Too many
times I am fooled, tricked, taken in. So here I am before You,
asking You to give me wisdom to see beyond facades. Reveal to
me what is real and what is not. And keep me alert to the wiles
of others so that I can tell the difference between the godly and
ungodly. In the meantime, I thank You, my God of peace, for
watching over me, protecting me, keeping me close and in Your
care, and loving me. In Jesus' name I pray. Amen.

Day 219

COMMUNITY

*I appeal to you, brothers and sisters, in the name of our
Lord Jesus Christ, that all of you agree with one another
in what you say and that there be no divisions among you,
but that you be perfectly united in mind and thought.*
1 CORINTHIANS 1:10

God, I realize that I want to pick the friends that I think I need,
and I confess that I don't always know what I need. Maybe what
I need is what You desire for me. I'm acknowledging that I grav-
itate toward people with whom I'm like-minded.

Would You please surprise me? Would You pick my friends for
me? Could I sense a connection, a stirring, and feel drawn to
those who You want me to reach out to, listen to? God, my desire is to be able to bring out who You are in every person I meet.

You created me with a longing for deep connection—with
You first, but with people as well. When it comes to community,
would You please be the one who invites those friends? May I
simply pay attention and say yes. In Jesus' name, amen.

Day 220
A FAITHFUL SERVANT

Master, you entrusted to me five talents; see, here I have gained five talents more. His master said to him, Well done, you upright (honorable, admirable) and faithful servant! You have been faithful and trustworthy over a little; I will put you in charge of much. Enter into and share the joy (the delight, the blessedness) which your master enjoys.
MATTHEW 25:20–21 AMPC

I want to be a good servant for You, Lord. I want to use the things with which You have gifted me, not hide them. So, dear Lord, give me the courage I need to step out for You. Help me nurture the talents You've given me then use them for the good of others and for Your glory. Show me what You would have me do, what You would want me to use to benefit Your kingdom. Help me to be faithful with what You have provided. I long for the day when we meet face-to-face. The day when You open Your arms to me and say, "Well done, My faithful daughter. Come to Me and share the joy and blessings waiting for you." Amen.

Day 221
A NEW HEART

*"I will give you a new heart and put a new spirit in you;
I will remove from you your heart of stone and give you
a heart of flesh. And I will put my Spirit in you and move
you to follow my decrees and be careful to keep my
laws. Then you will live in the land I gave your ancestors;
you will be my people, and I will be your God."*
EZEKIEL 36:26–28

Father, Pinocchio was a puppet carved from wood who wanted
to become a real boy. I also desire real life. I want a living heart
that's tender and responsive to Your urgings. Take away my
heart hardened by stubbornness and pride. Alone I can't quicken
a new heart, but You are the changer of hearts. Soften my heart
and fill me with Your Spirit. Without You, I'm a puppet to the
world's pleasures. Much like Pinocchio, I'm easily deceived into
thinking the false satisfaction of this earth will lead to something
lasting. But Your Spirit has cut my strings and given me
new life. I want to be called Yours. I want to carefully obey Your
ways. In Jesus' name, amen.

Day 222

THE IMPORTANT THING

I do not want to be proud of anything except in the cross of our Lord Jesus Christ. Because of the cross, the ways of this world are dead to me, and I am dead to them. If a person does or does not go through the religious act of becoming a Jew, it is worth nothing. The important thing is to become a new person. Those who follow this way will have God's peace and loving-kindness. They are the people of God.

GALATIANS 6:14–16 NLV

You have begun a new work in me, Lord. You, Your Son, and Your Spirit, as well as Your Word, have begun to transform me, to make me into a new woman, a woman of God. To get there from here, Lord, I need Your supernatural power and support, as well as some new strength every day. I need Your help as I learn to live and move in Your Spirit, to refresh, renew, and transform my mind, to sing this new song You have composed and planted in my heart. And I thank You for giving me Your peace and loving-kindness as I follow this way. In Jesus' name, amen.

Day 223
FOLLOW THROUGH

*Let your eyes look directly forward, and
your gaze be straight before you.*
PROVERBS 4:25 ESV

God, my brain is scattered. I can tell because I have clothes in various piles—on my chair, on the bed, on the floor. I haven't finished one thing well. I'm aware that this is a symptom of my scattered mind. I confess that I feel a bit topsy-turvy and in need of Your focused gaze.

Would You please look lovingly upon me? Would You please forgive me for where I attempt and don't follow through, where I start and don't finish? Would You give me grace to focus and have clarity and know where to put my time and attention in mind and heart?

As I focus, I want to hear Your voice. Would You please maximize those moments? Will You please celebrate when I accomplish one task at a time? I know that You meet me in the simplest ways when I still myself and slow down and follow through. In Jesus' name, amen.

Day 224
HELP AND SHIELD

*No king is saved by the power of his strong army.
A soldier is not saved by great strength. A horse cannot
be trusted to win a battle. Its great strength cannot
save anyone. . . . Our soul waits for the Lord. He is our
help and our safe cover. For our heart is full of joy in
Him, because we trust in His holy name. O Lord, let Your
loving-kindness be upon us as we put our hope in You.*
PSALM 33:16–17, 20–22 NLV

Lord, sometimes I grow impatient. Instead of waiting for You
to move, I find myself trusting in something other than You to
save me. I begin to scheme, to make plans, to search for my own
solutions. Yet those ideas never seem to work, and I just muck
things up even more, within and without. I realize I cannot rely
on anyone's strength but Yours, Lord. So please give me the gift
of patience. Help me to wait on You, my help and shield, knowing that You've got everything under control. Your timing is the
best. As I put my hope in You alone, my heart fills with joy. You
will work all things out for my good, here and beyond. Amen.

Day 225

ONE MORE DAY

This is the day the LORD has made.
We will rejoice and be glad in it.
PSALM 118:24 NLT

God, the sky is just beginning to awaken with the first glow of dawn. The birds are already cheering the rising sun with happy songs. The mist floats low over the fields as the first crimson rays filter through the trees. It's a new day! Yesterday is a memory and tomorrow but a hope, but today is here and with it a fresh start. A brand-new beginning. Another chance to praise You and do Your work. I will leave the mistakes and difficulties of yesterday in the past. Thank You, Jesus, for giving me another day to live for You. I will rejoice in this day because You made it and gifted it to me. May I use every waking moment of it for Your glory. Amen.

Day 226
GOD CALLING

God has called us to peace. For, wife, how can you
be sure of converting and saving your husband?
Husband, how can you be sure of converting and
saving your wife? Only, let each one [seek to conduct
himself and regulate his affairs so as to] lead the life
which the Lord has allotted and imparted to him and
to which God has invited and summoned him.
1 CORINTHIANS 7:15–17 AMPC

You have called me to a life of peace, Lord. But I need Your help. For that life of peace can be challenged by marriage. How I behave can draw my partner either toward You or away from You. So I'm going to need not only Your unlimited strength but Your wisdom. Lord, help me be a good example of a Christ follower. Help me lead the life You created me to lead, a life rich with peace, love, joy, understanding, and hope. Make me a woman who not only keeps her husband interested in her but leads him closer and closer to You. Abba God, Lord Jesus, and Holy Spirit, be with me as I answer Your call to peace. In Jesus' name, amen.

Day 227

WHAT I HAVE DONE FOR CHRIST

*But the LORD said to Samuel, "Do not look on his appearance
or on the height of his stature, because I have rejected
him. For the LORD sees not as man sees: man looks on the
outward appearance, but the LORD looks on the heart."*
1 SAMUEL 16:7 ESV

Much of my forgiveness journey is learning to forgive others
because *I've* been forgiven. I come to You today, repentant for
the daily ways I sin from my selfish desires.

Sin isn't something fun to sit in or think of. Yet, I'm asking You
to bring to mind what my sins are. Where am I selfish? Where
am I seeking validation? Where am I quick toward impatience
and judgment?

I'm listening and noticing what comes to mind. As these sins
surface, I'm asking for Your forgiveness. As I repent, I find myself less stuck in myself and more attuned to how You forgive so
that I can offer forgiveness.

Jesus, what have I done for You? Where have I listened to You?
Please talk to me about where I've selfishly pursued my own in-
terests, as well as times I've put myself aside and turned toward
You. Thank You, Jesus. Amen.

Day 228
HIDDEN TREASURE

"God's kingdom is like a treasure hidden in a field for years and then accidentally found by a trespasser. The finder is ecstatic—what a find!—and proceeds to sell everything he owns to raise money and buy that field. Or, God's kingdom is like a jewel merchant on the hunt for exquisite pearls. Finding one that is flawless, he immediately sells everything and buys it."
MATTHEW 13:44–46 MSG

I know my only path to joy, Lord Jesus, is to sacrifice all that I am and have so that I can gain Your kingdom. Through You, I can reach out to Father God, tap into His power, gain His blessing, get the guidance I need to do as He bids, and so much more. So help me, Jesus, to put You above all things. To seek You before all else. To turn to You upon waking in the morning and then just before I turn out the light at night. The only joy on earth is to be focused on You in heaven. To be in Your presence, feel Your embrace, and be showered by Your love and kindness. What a treasure! What a find! In Your name, I pray and rejoice. Amen.

Day 229
FILLED WITH GOD

I pray that you, being rooted and established in love, may have power, together with all the Lord's holy people, to grasp how wide and long and high and deep is the love of Christ, and to know this love that surpasses knowledge—that you may be filled to the measure of all the fullness of God.
EPHESIANS 3:17–19

Lord, You think big! It wasn't enough for You to create the world and set it spinning. You also planned in intricate detail how You would save us and spend all of eternity with us. But even that wasn't enough for Your ultimate plan. You also left us with Your Spirit to help and teach us. Filled to the measure of all the fullness of God—I can hardly imagine what that should look like. The total package of Your love, mercy, goodness, joy, and peace dwells within me as Your Holy Spirit. When I'm lacking patience, at my call is the fullness of Your patience. When my mood is flagging, Your abundant joy resides within me. Allow me to experience Your fullness today. In Jesus' name, amen.

Day 230
MY MAKER

Fear not, for you shall not be ashamed; neither be confounded and depressed, for you shall not be put to shame. For you shall forget the shame of your youth, and you shall not [seriously] remember the reproach of your widowhood any more. For your Maker is your Husband—the Lord of hosts is His name—and the Holy One of Israel is your Redeemer; the God of the whole earth He is called.
ISAIAH 54:4–5 AMPC

Life can be lonely, Lord, whether a person is married, single, or widowed. That's why I take such joy in looking to You to fulfill me in every way. You have claimed that You, my maker, are also my husband. You, the Lord of Hosts, are my Redeemer. You, the God of the whole earth, are also my Father, my beloved, my rock and refuge. Knowing You are all things to me, from *A* to *Z*, I will not fear nor be ashamed, confused, or depressed. Because You are my all in all, there is nothing else and no one else I need to feel complete, loved, and chosen. Thank You, my Savior, for loving me so. In Jesus' name, amen.

Day 231

NOTICING WHAT I OUGHT TO DO FOR JESUS

*So Jesus said to the Jews who had believed him,
"If you abide in my word, you are truly my disciples."*
JOHN 8:31 ESV

Where are You stirring and inviting me, Lord? As I think of Your self-sacrifice, bearing all sins, taking darkness upon Your body, dying so I can live, where are You asking me to live for You? What is it You created me to do in Your name? I realize my doing doesn't complete Your work but serves as a transformative testimony of Your forgiveness rooted in my obedience and action.

What ought I to do for You, Jesus? I'm listening. Where do I notice myself pulled and energized? Where do I feel obligated and tired? You are a Jesus of energy, not "shoulds." Anything churchy or legalistic or guilt-inducing is not what I ought to do for You. Instead, help me notice the "ought to" as an "I get to" invitation and confidently step into what You already began on the cross and will see to completion. Amen.

Day 232
VALLEY OF BLESSING

Jehoshaphat and his people came to take away what they wanted. . . . There was more than they could carry. It took them three days to take all the things, because there was so much. They gathered together in the Valley of Beracah [blessing] on the fourth day. There they praised and thanked the Lord. . . . They returned to Jerusalem with joy. For the Lord had filled them with joy by saving them.
2 Chronicles 20:25–27 nlv

How wonderful to know, Lord, that when I'm in trouble and I lay my problem down before You, ask for Your advice, and vow to do as You say, You move into action. You turn what seem like impossible situations into amazing victories. You turn curses into blessings. When I pray, You do things beyond my imagining. For there is nothing You cannot do. No problem You cannot fix. No curse You cannot undo. And before I know it, I find myself in the Valley of Blessing. Thank You, Lord, for not just saving me but championing me. For not just answering one prayer but thousands. For working in my life and filling me with irrepressible joy in You. Amen.

Day 233
INCREASED LOVE

*May the Lord make your love increase and overflow for each
other and for everyone else, just as ours does for you.*
1 THESSALONIANS 3:12

Father, thank You that I don't have to remain as I am. You continuously work to make me more like Jesus, and I can ask You for more of the things that I lack. I no longer have to believe the lie that "Oh, I'm just not an empathetic person" or "I'm not much of a servant." You can increase my love so that it rushes like a swollen creek in spring and overflows onto everyone around me. Increase my love today, Lord. Show me those in need of Your healing love, and let me be Your hands and feet. Reveal the dams in my life that are blocking the flow of Your love—selfishness, pride, bitterness—and remove them. In Jesus' name, amen.

Day 234

A FOREVER KIND OF LOVE

*"This exile is just like the days of Noah for me: I promised
then that the waters of Noah would never again flood
the earth. I'm promising now no more anger, no more
dressing you down. For even if the mountains walk away
and the hills fall to pieces, my love won't walk away
from you, my covenant commitment of peace won't fall
apart." The GOD who has compassion on you says so.*
ISAIAH 54:9–10 MSG

How soothing, how wonderful, how lovely to know, Lord, that
You have promised me a forever kind of love. Even if mountains are leveled and hills fall into the sea, You will continue to
love me. No matter what happens, Your covenant of peace will
neither be shaken nor fall apart. Your love for me, for all Your
daughters, is more than I can take in, Lord. There are very few
things in my life that are certain, and You, Lord, are one of them.
Thank You for loving me through the rough patches, for sticking
with me when all others deserted me. My love won't walk away
from You. Amen.

Day 235
TO SHINE

"You are the light of the world. A city set on a hill cannot be hidden. Nor do people light a lamp and put it under a basket, but on a stand, and it gives light to all in the house. In the same way, let your light shine before others, so that they may see your good works and give glory to your Father who is in heaven."
MATTHEW 5:14–16 ESV

Lord, why do I dim myself around certain people to be accepted or loved? This dimming is not from You. You created me to shine—not on my own to bring attention to myself but because Your glory is revealed through me. I ask for forgiveness for dimming, for shaming the deep, contemplative, big parts of me that I shrink small and quiet and closed off. Talk to me about why I do this. What would it look like to truly shine?

To live alive is to glorify You. How am I to forgive myself and others if I only offer the dimmed parts? Today I ask You to help me stand tall, to remove anything that threatens to dim and to move toward openness and vulnerability, to be a vessel of Your light. In Jesus' name, amen.

Day 236
SEEKING JESUS

Mary Magdalene and the other Mary went to see the tomb. . . . The angel said to the women, "Do not be afraid, for I know that you seek Jesus. . . . He is going before you to Galilee; there you will see him." . . . They departed quickly from the tomb with fear and great joy. . . . And behold, Jesus met them and said, "Greetings!" And they. . .worshiped him.
MATTHEW 28:1, 5, 7–9 ESV

Like the Marys, I too, Lord, am a female disciple. As such, I want to be as faithful to You as they were. Without fear, I look for You. With faith, I find You. And I'm never going to let You go. Be with me now. Help me look beyond myself and my assumptions and look to You and Your truth. I want to walk in Your will and way. To hear Your voice speak. To tell others where they can find You, what they can tell You, and how You will appear at the sound of our plea and prayer. Knowing that each day I can and will see You fills me with joy as I bow down at Your feet, ready to worship, to listen, to serve. In Your name, amen.

Day 237
EVER–PRESENT HELP

God is our refuge and strength, an ever-present help in trouble. Therefore we will not fear, though the earth give way and the mountains fall into the heart of the sea, though its waters roar and foam and the mountains quake with their surging. . . . The LORD Almighty is with us; the God of Jacob is our fortress.
PSALM 46:1–3, 7

God, sometimes my emotions overtake me at the smallest hiccups in my day—I broke my favorite dish or my car runs out of gas. Here I am upset over the little stuff when You have promised to keep me through much bigger problems than my chipped nail polish or failed dinner attempt. You promise to be my refuge if the mountains fall into the heart of the sea. I can admit that even my worst day hasn't approached a disaster of that magnitude. And even if my mountains aren't quite quaking, You still care about my problems. You are my ever-present help in trouble. I can call on the Lord Almighty at any time—even if it's only over a broken dish. Amen.

Day 238
PRAYING FOR PEACE

All your [spiritual] children shall be disciples [taught by the Lord and obedient to His will], and great shall be the peace and undisturbed composure of your children. You shall establish yourself in righteousness (rightness, in conformity with God's will and order): you shall be far from even the thought of oppression or destruction, for you shall not fear, and from terror, for it shall not come near you.
ISAIAH 54:13–14 AMPC

I long, Lord, for peace of mind, heart, body, soul, and spirit. And that's just what You promise not only for me but for the children of the future. So, Lord, today I pray that You would keep me far from danger. Remove from my mind any thoughts of destruction. Extract from my heart any bitterness that may darken its corridors. Silence my lips around disparaging remarks. Keep my hands from working plans away from You and my feet from walking roads away from You. And most of all, Lord, keep fear a far distance from me and courage intimately close. In Jesus' name I pray for such peace. Amen.

Day 239
CONFIDENCE IN THE UNSEEN

*Now faith is the assurance of things hoped
for, the conviction of things not seen.*
HEBREWS 11:1 ESV

God, I notice a pattern that I do well trusting when I see Your promises fulfilled, but when it's quiet or time goes by and there are no landmarks, I lose my footing and feel untethered and become scared. I doubt Your goodness.

I bring this to You, Jesus. I bring my doubt to You and ask for forgiveness. I wonder who else I do this with? When time goes by and I haven't connected with a friend, do I start to doubt our relationship? God, please forgive me when I'm so quick to forget, to lose confidence in You or a friendship when there's space or distance.

God, knowing this helps me be quick to forgive others when they are going through times when they need solidarity and my reaching out could be an encouragement to them. Please use my awareness of where I create distance and doubt to bring compassion and forgiveness to myself and others. In Jesus' name, amen.

Day 240
MY GOD, MY HELP

O send out Your light and Your truth, let them lead me. . .to Your dwelling. Then will I go to the altar of God, to God, my exceeding joy. . . . Why are you cast down, O my inner self? And why should you. . .be disquieted within me? Hope in God and wait expectantly for Him, for I shall yet praise Him, Who is the help of my [sad] countenance, and my God.
PSALM 43:3–5 AMPC

Lord, I come to Your Word. Send Your light out to me. Allow it to reveal the truth You would have me know. Let the light of Your Word lead me into Your presence, the place where I find my peace, feel Your touch, and experience unfathomable joy. Calm my soul, Lord. Erase my anxiety. Be the balm to my inner self. Renew my hope, Lord. Help me to wait for You, to expect Your goodness to meet my prayer. Give me these moments of quiet. Make my spirit as calm as still water. And as I rest here with You, I give You all my praise and the joy that comes with it. Amen.

Day 241
A WAY MAKER

This is what the LORD says—he who made a way through the sea, a path through the mighty waters. . . . "Forget the former things; do not dwell on the past. See, I am doing a new thing! Now it springs up; do you not perceive it? I am making a way in the wilderness and streams in the wasteland."
ISAIAH 43:16, 18–19

Lord, I've been lost in what seems like impossible circumstances. My anxiety builds as I turn every facet and examine every possibility only to find every avenue closed to me. There seems to be no escape. I feel like the Israelites, backs to the sea, facing an army of chariots. But then I remember that You made a way where there was none before. My mortal eyes may not perceive Your workings, but I know that You are the way maker. You rolled back the waves and the Israelites passed through to a new land. You can spring up streams in my wasteland and blaze a way through my wilderness. Meet me here in my desert and lead me home. In the name of Jesus, amen.

Day 242
BLINDINGLY OBVIOUS

Be cheerful. Keep things in good repair. Keep your spirits up. Think in harmony. Be agreeable. Do all that, and the God of love and peace will be with you for sure. Greet one another with a holy embrace. All the brothers and sisters here say hello. The amazing grace of the Master, Jesus Christ, the extravagant love of God, the intimate friendship of the Holy Spirit, be with all of you.
2 CORINTHIANS 13:11–14 MSG

Lord, I want to do what You would have me do, to follow Your lead in all things. Yet oftentimes I am going to need Your help, for some things don't come to me as naturally as they do for others. So, as I walk this road with You, Lord, help me to have an optimistic outlook. To see and focus on the good in all things and people, even if the not-so-good is blindingly obvious. Help me encourage others, including myself, by planting good words and seeds of love in their midst. Give me a mind that thinks with compassion, not conflict. And as I do these things, Lord, may it be blindingly obvious to others that You, the God of peace and love, are with me. Amen.

Day 243
RESENTFUL FEELINGS

*Love is patient and kind; love does not envy or boast;
it is not arrogant or rude. . . . Love bears all things,
believes all things, hopes all things, endures all things.*
1 CORINTHIANS 13:4–5, 7 ESV

I'm resentful today. I'm resentful of the love I've poured into people and not felt like it has come back. I'm resentful of the hard work I've invested and not seen the fruit of my labor. I'm resentful for trusting You and not seeing the next step. Jesus, I offer all my resentments to You.

I acknowledge these resentments and ask for Your forgiveness. This reminds me to ask You: Are there any resentments You have with me? Are there resentments people have with me? Are there ways people have poured into me that I haven't offered back, or said thank you, or been gracious or generous, or acknowledged their efforts?

Today, I surrender resentment. Thank You for forgiving the resentment I carry; would this not root into bitterness, but may this be a draw to live resentment-free and full of grace. In Jesus' name, amen.

Day 244
A GREAT LIGHT

Gloom will not be upon her who is distressed. . . .
The people who walked in darkness have seen a great
light. . . . Upon them a light has shined. . . . They rejoice
before You. . . . For unto us a Child is born, unto us a Son is
given. . . . And His name will be called Wonderful, Counselor,
Mighty God, Everlasting Father, Prince of Peace.
ISAIAH 9:1–3, 6 NKJV

When the shadows of sadness come upon me, Lord, rise up. Shine Your light down upon me. Break up the gloom that threatens to envelop me. Expel the darkness so that I may rejoice in Your Son-shine. You are the wonder of my life. You have the guidance I need to walk Your way. Deliver me with Your mighty power. Counsel me with Your wisdom. Let no one snatch me out of Your hand. Be my forever Father, my shield, my protector, my Abba God. Be the priceless Prince with whom I live happily ever after in this world and the next. Lord, surround me with Your peace, love, grace, and mercy as I abide in You. In Jesus' name, amen.

Day 245
HE NEVER GIVES UP

*But our citizenship is in heaven. And we eagerly
await a Savior from there, the Lord Jesus Christ, who,
by the power that enables him to bring everything
under his control, will transform our lowly bodies
so that they will be like his glorious body.*
PHILIPPIANS 3:20–21

Father, soften the hard clay of my heart so that it is yielded to Your sculpting hand on my life. Help me to heed Your Holy Spirit's urgings. You are the master artist who would mold my heart into something beautiful if I surrender my will to Yours. I'm so grateful that You don't give up on me. Even when I falter and stray from You, You're capable of redeeming my poor choices and making me more like Jesus. I look ahead toward heaven, my true home, and the things of this world shift into proper perspective. They're temporary. They're shallow. They're distractions. Give me eyes that see and ears that hear as You continue to do the good work in me that You started. Amen.

Day 246

WITHIN YOUR WALLS

I was glad when they said to me, "Let us go to the house of the Lord." . . . May all go well for those who love you. May there be peace within your walls. May all go well within your houses. I will now say, "May peace be within you," for the good of my brothers and my friends. Because of the house of the Lord our God, I will pray for your good.
PSALM 122:1, 6–9 NLV

Something happens to me, Lord, when I come into Your house, when I step into Your sanctuary, Your place of peace. That's when I am most conscious of Your world totally surrounding me—my walls within Yours and Your walls within mine. Me in You and You in me is a safe place to be in a world often fraught with conflict. Help me, Lord, to carry that sense of place and peace within myself so that wherever I am, my connection to You is firm and sure. And as I appropriate Your peace, Lord, and make it my own, give me the opportunity to share it with others and bless them with peace within their walls, houses, and deep within. May Your peace reign. Amen.

Day 247
A PASTURE EXPERIENCE

*The LORD is my shepherd; I shall not want. He makes
me lie down in green pastures. He leads me beside still
waters. He restores my soul. He leads me in paths of
righteousness for his name's sake. . . . Surely goodness
and mercy shall follow me all the days of my life,
and I shall dwell in the house of the LORD forever.*

PSALM 23:1–3, 6 ESV

God, when I read Psalm 23, I am drawn to the visual of a pasture.
How I long to create that safe, soul-nourishing space. A place
where I can come and be fully known and fully loved and find
Your gentle care.

Where have You made me lie down to rest? Where are You
walking beside still waters with me? What are those times in the
darkest valley, and where have I noticed Your comfort?

God, I'm asking for Your provision as I make my home a pasture—a safe space where all who enter will come to know You
and find truth and grace.

I know forgiveness is a part of traveling along the pasture.
Thank You for meeting me there. Help me create a pasture experience wherever I am. Amen.

Day 248
EYE-OPENER

They began to recognize God and praise and give thanks. . . . God has visited His people [in order to help and care for and provide for them]! And this report concerning [Jesus] spread. . . . In that very hour Jesus was healing many [people] of sicknesses and distressing bodily plagues and evil spirits, and to many who were blind He gave [a free, gracious, joy-giving gift of] sight.
LUKE 7:16–17, 21 AMPC

I am still amazed, Father God, by the gift You have given me in Your Son, Jesus. Through Him, You came and walked among us. You are and have been my helper, caretaker, and provider. You heal me from the sickness within my body, mind, spirit, and soul. You de-stress me, taking away my cares, woes, anxieties, and issues. You have opened my eyes to the truth of Your Word. Through that lens, I see the path You want me to take, the road You want me to travel. Thank You for the joy-giving gift of Jesus, the one who continually opens my eyes, mind, and heart so that I can see You. In His name, I pray, amen.

Day 249
HE DOES THE IMPOSSIBLE

*This is the confidence we have in approaching God:
that if we ask anything according to his will, he hears
us. And if we know that he hears us—whatever we
ask—we know that we have what we asked of him.*
1 JOHN 5:14–15

God, sometimes I underestimate Your awesome power. I ask for things but don't really expect You to move. It seems impossible to change things. When the apostle Peter was in prison for preaching Your gospel, the believers gathered in an all-night prayer vigil, and You showed up in a huge way. You sent an angel to release Peter from prison—dropped his chains and walked him right out the gate! Yet when Peter showed up at the house, the believers were shocked by his arrival. They expected so much less from You. Give me faith that when I pray according to Your will, You will answer in big ways. Shock me with Your power to bring about the seemingly impossible. In Jesus' name, amen.

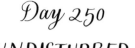

Day 250

UNDISTURBED

May grace (God's unmerited favor) and spiritual peace [which means peace with God and harmony, unity, and undisturbedness] be yours from God our Father and from the Lord Jesus Christ. . . . You who once were [so] far away, through (by, in) the blood of Christ have been brought near. For He is [Himself] our peace (our bond of unity and harmony).
EPHESIANS 1:2; 2:13–14 AMPC

Grace, favor, peace, harmony, unity, undisturbedness, brought near—the beauty of these words, Lord, leaves me breathless. In these days, these words seem rarely used, for they are not reflective of the atmosphere in which we now live. And that is why I seek You, why I love delving into Your Word, why I continually plant Your good news within my heart. Today, Lord, pour down upon me, refresh me with Your grace and peace. Draw me ever closer so that I may feel Your presence and take in Your energy, life, and light. You—God, Jesus, Spirit—are my peace, my path, my passion, my provision. Keep me by Your side, undisturbed by the woes of the world, knowing You alone *are* my world. In Jesus' name I pray. Amen.

Day 251

SOULFUL CONVERSATION

Whoever walks with the wise becomes wise,
but the companion of fools will suffer harm.
PROVERBS 13:20 ESV

God, I'm in need of some good deep, soulful conversation. I confess that small talk makes my soul wither. Deep connection though? It feels like a big gulp of air. Deep, knowing air. For years I lived in the shallow end, forfeiting the deep waters for only small surfacy conversation, but now that I've tasted depth and authenticity, I crave these connections more and more.

God, in my desire for soul conversations, forgive me for dreading small talk. Help me realize that not everyone desires depth and emotions and vulnerability; help me to be okay meeting people where they are. In turn, I ask You to bring those who desire depth and spiritual conversations to my path and to hold both in balance with Your Spirit. In Jesus' name, amen.

Day 252
GOOD NEWS

There were shepherds in the fields. They were watching their flocks of sheep at night. The angel of the Lord came to them. The shining-greatness of the Lord shone around them. They were very much afraid. The angel said to them, "Do not be afraid. See! I bring you good news of great joy which is for all people. Today, One Who saves from the punishment of sin has been born. . . . He is Christ the Lord."
LUKE 2:8–11 NLV

I love how You gave Your Son's birth announcement to human-kind, Lord. You directed angels to proclaim the great news, the good news, about Jesus to a simple band of shepherds, socially considered one of the lowest groups of people. The angel's first words to them were "Don't be afraid. I've got some good news that's going to bring you great happiness. Jesus, God's Son, will save you!" When *I* first heard Your news, it seemed too good to be true—that someone sacrificed all so that I could live for You, see You, pray to You. Yet that good news was, still is, and forever will be true. Thank You for the joy I find in Jesus, Your Son and my Lord, King, and Savior. Amen.

Day 253
THE REAL DEAL

"I am the LORD, and there is no other. I have not spoken in secret, from somewhere in a land of darkness; I have not said to Jacob's descendants, 'Seek me in vain.' I, the LORD, speak the truth. . . . Ignorant are those who carry about idols of wood, who pray to gods that cannot save. . . . Turn to me and be saved. . .for I am God, and there is no other."
ISAIAH 45:18–20, 22

Lord, You are the God who created the heavens and fashioned the earth. There are no substitutes for You. And yet we humans have tried so hard for millennia to carve out our own forged gods. They're powerless, and yet we give them our attention and devotion as if they cared about us in return, as You do. You created this fantastic and beautiful planet especially for us, Your ultimate creation. You wanted a relationship with us so completely that You sent Your Son to die for us. Show me any weak substitutes I've replaced You with. Reveal the things I use for comfort and security instead of seeking You. I want more of You, God. You are the I Am. There is no other. Amen.

Day 254
FROM THE HEART

I ask you from my heart to live and work the way the Lord expected you to live and work. Live and work without pride. Be gentle and kind. Do not be hard on others. Let love keep you from doing that. Work hard to live together as one by the help of the Holy Spirit. Then there will be peace.
EPHESIANS 4:1–3 NLV

Lord, I'm looking not just for peace within, although that's where it begins, but for peace without. For peace between me and the next man or woman. So, Lord, please show me; lead me to what You want me to do, how You want me to live. Fill my head, hands, and heart with the inspiration I need to do what You've called me to do, to work as You've called me to work, to live as You would have me live. Put pride far from me, and bring gentleness and kindness in close. Help me to treat others with compassion and love, just like I'd want to be treated. And above all, Lord, give myself and my fellow believers the aid and unity of Your Holy Spirit so we can live as one, in one, for one, in peace. In Jesus' name I pray. Amen.

Day 255
FINISHING WHAT I START

*Better is the end of a thing than its beginning, and the
patient in spirit is better than the proud in spirit.*
ECCLESIASTES 7:8 ESV

God, I get so excited and passionate and all-in, and then I lose energy to finish well. I lose the spark to follow through. I hate this about me. Why do I do this, God? What is at the root of my lack of follow-through? Do I feel like I need to do it perfectly? Do I feel like it doesn't really matter?

Would You please help me pay attention to why it is that I have trouble finishing some projects? What is this resistance in me? God, please forgive me for starting well and not finishing.

Today, would You please help me follow through and complete one task well? Would You help me sift through where to put my energy? Will You please walk along with me until I complete this? May I sense how You are noting what I do finish instead of shaming me for what's not yet done. You are a Father who sees the good and longs for me to be proud of my work, just as You are proud of me. Amen.

Day 256

THE VOICE OF JOY

Show your happiness, all peoples! Call out to God with
the voice of joy! For the Lord Most High is to be feared.
He is a great King over all the earth. He sets people under
us, and nations under our feet. He chooses for us what
is to be ours, the pride of Jacob, whom He loves. . . .
God rules over the nations. God sits on His holy throne.
PSALM 47:1–4, 8 NLV

It seems so easy, Lord, for me to get weighed down by world news. I sometimes feel so helpless, unable to stop the tide of evil. Yet that's not how You would have me be. For I'm Your child. You're my King, the one who rules over all things, who chooses what I am to be and have in this life. You want me to be filled with joy. What kind of witness for You would I be if I were constantly worried, frightened, upset, and anxious? So, Lord, today, right here, right now, turn my frown upside down! Give me that deep sense of joy from which I can draw—no matter what's happening within and without. In Jesus' name I pray and praise, amen.

Day 257
HE RESTORES

The LORD is my shepherd, I lack nothing.
He makes me lie down in green pastures, he leads
me beside quiet waters, he refreshes my soul.
PSALM 23:1–3

Lord, I'm tired, worn out, and beaten down. I'm exhausted from fighting the same old battles every day. I'm emotionally on edge and about to graduate to hot mess. I'm not sure I can stay in this war another day. But I know that You give strength to the weary and rest to the burdened. You are a compassionate and tender God who cares for me. Instead of losing patience with my toddler-worthy tired attitude, You lovingly lead me to the rest and restoration that I need. You restore me to strength and refresh my perspective. Thank You for providing for all my needs—both physical and spiritual. Show me how to deal kindly with others when they need refreshment. In the name of Jesus, amen.

Day 258
THE SEARCH

I know the thoughts and plans that I have for you, says the Lord, thoughts and plans for welfare and peace and not for evil, to give you hope in your final outcome. Then you will call upon Me, and you will come and pray to Me, and I will hear and heed you. Then you will seek Me, inquire for, and require Me [as a vital necessity] and find Me when you search for Me with all your heart.
JEREMIAH 29:11–13 AMPC

Lord, I know You have plans for me. Yet I feel I'm not where I thought I'd be at this point in my life. I expected something different, perhaps something better. And I'm a bit concerned over what lies ahead. So help me, Lord, to trust You with my future. For I know You have thought and planned for me since before I was a twinkle in my father's eye or a smile on my mother's lips. You have prepared a good outcome for me, for peace in my life and not evil, all so that I will have hope in my future. Open my ears to Your Word, open my soul to Your love, open my spirit to Your peace as I search for You with all of my heart. Amen.

Day 259
AN ACTIVE FAITH

*Now faith is the assurance of things hoped
for, the conviction of things not seen.*
HEBREWS 11:1 ESV

God, faith is a funny thing. Because faith lived with You is unpredictable and unknown. Active faith embodies mystery and awe and wonder; it is not calculated or comfortable. Yet, the enemy lies and tells us that if we're faithful, blessings abound, and I'm finding this not to be true.

When I look back in scripture and see Your faithful followers, those who lived an active faith, they suffered a ton. They laid down everything to follow You. God, I ask for Your forgiveness as I am often frustrated by what it looks like to live an active faith.

Active faith requires stepping into the uncomfortable, surrendering my ego. Active faith requires putting aside my desires to come alongside Your will. Lord, help me step into a life of active faith. Please forgive me for what I'm still holding on to. Please offer hope glimmers of what it looks like to take up Your cross and live a life of action, a life of faithfulness, a life of ongoing trust, even when it's scary and uncomfortable. In Jesus' name, amen.

Day 260

THE HABIT OF JOYFUL HOPE

Let us. . .rejoice in our sufferings, knowing that pressure and affliction and hardship produce patient and unswerving endurance. And endurance (fortitude) develops maturity of character (approved faith and tried integrity). And character [of this sort] produces [the habit of] joyful and confident hope of eternal salvation. Such hope never disappoints or deludes or shames us, for God's love has been poured out in our hearts through the Holy Spirit Who has been given to us.
ROMANS 5:3–5 AMPC

Even when I feel as if I'm going through the wringer, Lord, I have hope. For Your Word tells me that my troubles are actually good for me. They strengthen me. They bring me back to You. They remind me of the joy I have because I know I will one day be with You in heaven forever. And it is that hope that keeps me going, looking to You, feeling Your love bloom within me through the Holy Spirit You've given me. Within You, Lord, I have all I need not just to get through this life but to experience Your abundant peace and provision amid the process. Amen.

Day 261
LIVING BREAD

"I am the bread of life. Your ancestors ate the manna in the wilderness, yet they died. But here is the bread that comes down from heaven, which anyone may eat and not die. I am the living bread that came down from heaven. Whoever eats this bread will live forever. This bread is my flesh, which I will give for the life of the world."
JOHN 6:48–51

Father, we eat our fill and satisfy our hunger only to hear our stomachs grumble for more in a few short hours. Our physical bodies burn through food and crave more, always more. Spiritually, we have the same insatiable appetite. I've tried to satisfy it with the junk food of society. I've consumed the world's buffet of living for myself, being good, obtaining money, but after a while I feel empty again. But You, Jesus, are the bread of life. Living bread that fills all my voids and never leaves me hungry. Since I've found You, I don't need to return again and again to the world's table, looking for that something to satisfy me. In You I have found what my soul craves. Amen.

Day 262
ROUND ABOUT

*Those who trust in, lean on, and confidently hope in
the Lord are like Mount Zion, which cannot be moved
but abides and stands fast forever. As the mountains
are round about Jerusalem, so the Lord is round about
His people from this time forth and forever. . . .
Do good, O Lord, to those who are good, and to those
who are right [with You and all people] in their hearts.*
PSALM 125:1–2, 4 AMPC

When I'm unsettled, frightened, unsure, stressed, worried, and
overwhelmed, I run to You, Lord. For You are the one person,
the one Spirit, the one God above all gods I trust. Others lean
on humans. But humans are fallible. That's why I lean on You and
hope in You alone. You, like Mount Zion, cannot be moved. You
will be and always have been there for me, holding me, helping
me. Like the mountains that surround and protect Jerusalem,
You surround and protect me. And You've promised to do so
forever and ever. So as I come to You today, Lord, as I lean into
Your loving arms, surround me with Your love, protection, and
peace. Shield me from this foreign land until I arrive back home
with You. Amen.

Day 263
UNTAPPED PASSION

*Each of you should use whatever gift you have
received to serve others, as faithful stewards
of God's grace in its various forms.*
1 PETER 4:10

Jesus, You know my prayer before it even leaves my lips. You created me with much passion and heart to come alongside how You are moving in and through me. I confess, I'm not sure what to do with this passion. I feel untapped, like a teakettle about to sing at the top of my lungs. I feel pent-up and about to burst.

What do I do with this untapped passion? How am I to use it? Where are You asking me to be still and wait? Where do You want me to act? How do I glorify You through these passions?

Lord, in my lack of answers and uber-passionate soul, may I obediently take one step toward where You are moving. Just one step. And then another for the next day. May I find nourishment in Your daily bread and trust that You are revealing a reason for these gifts and that You will not let them go to waste. Amen.

Day 264
OCCUPIED WITH JOY

What I have seen to be good and fitting is to eat and drink and find enjoyment in all the toil with which one toils under the sun the few days of his life that God has given him, for this is his lot. Everyone also to whom God has given wealth and possessions and power to enjoy them, and to accept his lot and rejoice in his toil—this is the gift of God. For he will not much remember the days of his life because God keeps him occupied with joy in his heart.
ECCLESIASTES 5:18–20 ESV

This is what I want, Lord. To enjoy the life You have given me. To enjoy whatever I eat and drink and whatever work I put my hand to. For this is the life with which You have so wonderfully blessed me. I want to be so focused on all the good things in my life, so content with what You have gifted me, that I don't get hung up on the negative things. I don't want to allow the world's woes to put a shadow upon my blessings from You. Keep me occupied, Lord, with all the joy You have already planted in my heart today and every day. Amen.

Day 265
PURSUED

For day and night your hand was heavy on me;
my strength was sapped as in the heat of summer.
Then I acknowledged my sin to you and did not cover
up my iniquity. I said, "I will confess my transgressions
to the LORD." And you forgave the guilt of my sin.
PSALM 32:4–5

Lord, King David tried to cover up his sin, but that led only to more sin. And You didn't let him get away with it. He probably should have known that hiding was futile. People might not discover what he'd done, but You see right into our hearts and know all. When I do wrong, my natural inclination is also to pull a cover-up job. But You love me too much to let me slide into sin unhindered. Like the dense weight of the summer heat, when walking out of my air-conditioning feels like smacking into concrete, Your hand of conviction presses upon me until I tire of running and turn to You. And when I confess, I experience the cool relief of Your forgiveness. Amen.

Day 266

BLESSED QUIET FOR YOUR SOUL

Come to Me, all you who labor and are heavy-laden and overburdened, and I will cause you to rest. [I will ease and relieve and refresh your souls.] Take My yoke upon you and learn of Me, for I am gentle (meek) and humble (lowly) in heart, and you will find rest (relief and ease and refreshment and recreation and blessed quiet) for your souls.
MATTHEW 11:28–29 AMPC

Lord, I come to You in this moment, my back aching from the load I've been carrying. It's too much for me to bear. So I leave it at Your feet. Please, Jesus, give me the relief I so desperately need. Help me recover my life, my heart, my soul from the pressures of this world. Lead me to Your kingdom so that I can find the relief and ease I need. Show me, Lord, how to take a real break, a real rest. Help me get back into Your rhythm, to walk in step with You, to take a deep breath and relax, and to allow You to replace my problems with Your peace. Bless my soul, Jesus, with Your quiet. Amen.

Day 267
INTO HIS KEEPING

[The jailer]. . .fell down before Paul and Silas. . . .
Men, what is it necessary for me to do that I may be
saved? And they answered, Believe in the Lord Jesus Christ
[give yourself up to Him, take yourself out of your own
keeping and entrust yourself into His keeping] and you
will be saved, [and this applies both to] you and your
household as well. . . . Then he. . .leaped much for joy.
ACTS 16:29–31, 34 AMPC

So often, Lord, I find that I really haven't given You all of me. I attempt to take care of myself, to trust my own skills, resources, and knowledge. I actually think I know better than You! Today, Jesus, make me a woman totally in Your keeping. Help me give You all of me, to leave nothing behind. To entrust all things to You—my mind, body, soul, spirit, family, friends, country, possessions, present, and future. Remind me of Your power, grace, forgiveness, and wisdom. Help me get it through my head that only by taking myself out of my own keeping and into Yours will I find the joy that will make me want to leap, to dance, to sing in Your name. Amen.

Day 268
OPEN MINDS

At that, Jesus rejoiced, exuberant in the Holy Spirit.
"I thank you, Father, Master of heaven and earth, that you
hid these things from the know-it-alls and showed them to
these innocent newcomers. Yes, Father, it pleased you to
do it this way." . . . He then turned in a private aside to his
disciples. "Fortunate the eyes that see what you're seeing."
LUKE 10:21, 23 MSG

Your Word is so precious to me, Lord. The fact that I can pick up my Bible and read about You is amazing. Once I too was a vast wasteland, and then You and Your Word hovered over me. You said, "Let there be light," and I saw the truth for the first time. I heard Your voice speak deep into my spirit. Help me never take for granted the fact that through Your Word I can see how You have been moving. Thank You for letting me read, see, and hear Your story from Genesis to Revelation, for opening my simple mind to the power of Your Word. Every page I turn, every passage I read, prompts me to rejoice in spirit, soul, mind, and heart. Amen.

Day 269
MY CHAMPION

*"You have seen with your own eyes all that the LORD your God
has done to these two kings. The LORD will do the same to
all the kingdoms over there where you are going. Do not be
afraid of them; the LORD your God himself will fight for you."*
DEUTERONOMY 3:21–22

Lord, I know You've got my back when I'm walking in Your will.
You promised to fight the Israelites' battles for them if they
would obey You and trust in Your promises. You'll fight mine too
if I step out in faith in the direction You're nudging me. After
all, if You are for me, who can be against me? No one can stand
against the mighty God of creation who holds all power and
knowledge in the palm of His hand. Give me faith to go where
You lead and see what You will do. You have brought down city
walls and sent enemy armies fleeing in terror. I don't have to fear
when You are the champion of my cause. In Jesus' name, amen.

Day 270

LOOKING UP

If then you have been raised with Christ [to a new life, thus sharing His resurrection from the dead], aim at and seek the [rich, eternal treasures] that are above, where Christ is, seated at the right hand of God. And set your minds and keep them set on what is above (the higher things), not on the things that are on the earth. For [as far as this world is concerned] you have died, and your [new, real] life is hidden with Christ in God.
COLOSSIANS 3:1–3 AMPC

I'm losing my peace, Lord, and I think it's because my eyes are in the wrong place. It seems I've been focusing on everything *except* for You. Help me raise my sights, Lord. Lift my head so I can seek the things that are above this earth, the forever riches I have in knowing You and Your Son. Lift my eyes and mind, Lord, so that I may see the higher things, such as peace, love, understanding, compassion, empathy, and wisdom. Each day, lift my thoughts, Lord, ever higher. Transform my mind, shape my thoughts, so that each day I may become more like Jesus, my hero, Savior, and Prince of Peace. In His name I pray, amen.

Day 271
WORD WELCOMED

They answered, Believe in the Lord Jesus Christ. . . . And they declared the Word of the Lord. . . . And he took them the same hour of the night and bathed [them because of their bloody] wounds. . . . Then he took them up into his house and set food before them; and he leaped much for joy and exulted with all his family that he believed in God [accepting and joyously welcoming what He had made known through Christ].
ACTS 16:31–34 AMPC

Oh gentlest of saviors, how much You still have to teach me. I *do* believe in You. I put myself entirely in Your keeping, leaving no remainder behind to fret or fear. And then I read Your Word, and my eyes are opened, my heart moved. Your gentleness prompts me to be gentle to others—the chained, injured, and lost. To pull them close to me and to tend to their wounds. To share what I have with them. As Your Word fills every crevice of want and desire, I am led to You, Your power, Your grace, Your love, and Your light, which then flow through me and onto others. Your Word is more than welcome in my life, Lord. It *is* my life. Amen.

Day 272
A QUENCHED THIRST

O God, You are my God. I will look for You with all my heart and strength. My soul is thirsty for You. My flesh is weak wanting You in a dry and tired land where there is no water. . . . I have seen Your power and Your shining-greatness. . . . I will lift up my hands in Your name. My soul will be filled. . . . And my mouth praises You with lips of joy.
PSALM 63:1–2, 4–5 NLV

Oh Lord, my God, I need You. I need Your presence, Your cooling shade, Your warming arms. You are everything I desire and thirst for. I am desperate for Your comfort and love. Give me some good news through Your Word. Show me Your power and might. Imbue me with Your love and grace. Draw me out of myself and into Your presence. Here alone do I find my source, my provision, my strength, my refuge. In You I am home. In You I have hope. I'm lifting up my hands, Lord, to praise and worship You. Fill my soul with Your Spirit, and my mouth will respond with praises of joy. In Jesus' name, amen.

Day 273
PATH TO ETERNITY

"Blessed are the poor in spirit, for theirs is the kingdom of heaven. Blessed are those who mourn, for they will be comforted. Blessed are the meek, for they will inherit the earth. Blessed are those who hunger and thirst for righteousness, for they will be filled."
MATTHEW 5:3–6

God, our future is full of hope—the promise of an eternal place of peace with You. Thank You, Jesus, for pointing us toward the road that leads to heaven. Thank You for walking up a mountainside and sitting down to teach the masses how to live in Your kingdom. You said we're blessed when we recognize our spiritual bankruptcy before a holy God. You promised to comfort those who grieve over the sins they have committed against You. And those who clearly recognize their humble position will inherit everything. When we realize our great need for You and hunger and thirst to know more of You, You will satisfy us with the bread of life and living water. In the name of Jesus, amen.

Day 274
BY HEART

Do not forget my teaching. Let your heart keep my words. For they will add to you many days and years of life and peace. Do not let kindness and truth leave you. Tie them around your neck. Write them upon your heart. So you will find favor and good understanding in the eyes of God and man.
PROVERBS 3:1–4 NLV

When I'm confused and unsettled, Lord, lead me into Your Word. Show me what You would have me know. And when I've understood, when I've applied Your Word to my life, help me to not just take Your teaching to heart but to learn it by heart. I have discovered the power of Your Word. When I recall Your verses that I've stored in my mind, they wield so much force and emit so much strength within and without that I can't help but find myself amazed. And once the amazement fades, I'm left with joy and peace—joy that You have once more rescued me and peace that You have once more been there for me. Today, Lord, continue my education. Lead me to Your next teaching and the next words to write on my heart. Amen.

Day 275

HOME ONCE MORE

Some sat in darkness and in the shadow of death.
They suffered in prison in iron chains. Because they had
turned against the Words of God. . . . Then they cried out to
the Lord in their trouble. And He saved them. . . .
He brought them out of darkness and the shadow of
death. And He broke their chains. . . . Let them give Him
gifts of thanks and tell of His works with songs of joy.
PSALM 107:10–11, 13–14, 22 NLV

Even when I go against Your Word, Lord, You save me. Even when my own stubbornness leads me away from Your will and toward my own, You hear my cry. When all around is darkness, You bring me back out into the light of Your way. You break the ties that have bound me. And once again I am humbled. I can barely look up at You. For although I am full of joy that I am back in Your shadow, I am full of shame. Why am I so willful? Forgive me, Lord. Pull me into Your compassionate embrace. Hold me tight as I snuggle back into Your warmth, so glad to be home with You once more. Amen.

Day 276

MOVED WITH COMPASSION

When he came to himself, he said. . . . I will get up and go to my father, and I will say to him, Father, I have sinned. . . . While he was still a long way off, his father saw him and was moved with pity and tenderness [for him]; and he ran and embraced him and kissed him [fervently]. . . . The father said. . . . Let us revel and feast and be happy and make merry.
LUKE 15:17–18, 20, 22–23 AMPC

Sometimes, Lord, I don't realize how far I have strayed from You. But then when I come to myself, I know what I have to say. I have to tell You, in my own words, how I have erred and made a misstep. Help me right here and now ask for Your forgiveness. Help me to picture You as a Father who is looking for me, waiting for me, even when I'm still a long way off. Let me see You as a Father who is moved with love and compassion for me. Open Your arms, Lord, as I turn this corner and run into Your embrace. Grant me Your forgiveness. And may we end this moment by reveling in each other's company, full of joy, feasting on our mutual love. Amen.

Day 277
TENDER SHEPHERD

Jesus went through all the towns and villages, teaching in their synagogues, proclaiming the good news of the kingdom and healing every disease and sickness. When he saw the crowds, he had compassion on them, because they were harassed and helpless, like sheep without a shepherd.
MATTHEW 9:35–36

Father, sometimes I entertain the wrong image of You. I think that You condemn me, that You're waiting for me to mess up so You can punish me for each and every failure. That I have to be perfect in order to be accepted by You. But I don't have to put on my Sunday clothes for You. I couldn't even if I tried. You don't look upon me with censure and anger and impatience as I stumble along after You; You see me with eyes of compassion. You know that I'm harassed and helpless, a lamb in need of a strong and caring shepherd. Thank You, Jesus, for Your compassionate care of me. You have guided me into healing and abundant life in Your kingdom. Amen.

Day 278

VIBRANT HARMONIES

From beginning to end he's there, towering far above everything, everyone. So spacious is he, so expansive, that everything of God finds its proper place in him without crowding. Not only that, but all the broken and dislocated pieces of the universe—people and things, animals and atoms—get properly fixed and fit together in vibrant harmonies, all because of his death, his blood that poured down from the cross.
COLOSSIANS 1:18–20 MSG

Jesus, my Lord and Savior, when I think of all You went through to save someone like me, I am very humbled and grateful. For it was through Your innocent blood shed on the cross that our Father made His peace with us. All the broken bits, all the loose ends, all the creatures and creations in the universe were made whole and complete once more through You. Because of You, everything has now been repaired, remade, renewed, and refreshed. All is in harmony because of Your death. Yet because You still live, because I still have access to You, I also have access to Your peace. Help me, Lord, to live a life in tune with You. Amen.

Day 279

ENJOYING THE DAYS

I know that it will be well for those who fear God. . . .
But it will not go well for the sinful. . . . There are right
and good men who have the same thing happen to them
that happens to those who do sinful things. And there
are sinful men who have the same thing happen to them
that happens to those who are right and good. . . .
So I say a man should enjoy himself. . . . Eat and drink and
be happy. . . . Through the days. . .which God has given him.
ECCLESIASTES 8:12–15 NLV

I keep waiting, Lord, for bad people to "get theirs." But they never seem to! And Your Word says that's just how it is. Sometimes bad things happen to good people, and good things happen to bad people. At least on earth, anyway. So help me, Lord, to turn all these thoughts over to You. To realize I'll never be able to figure everything out. But You have and will take care of it. Meanwhile, I'm going to enjoy my days with You, right here, right now. I'm going to live and be joy filled in Your name. Amen!

Day 280
AT HOME IN GOD

Silence is praise to you, Zion-dwelling God, and also obedience. You hear the prayer in it all. We all arrive at your doorstep sooner or later, loaded with guilt, our sins too much for us—but you get rid of them once and for all. Blessed are the chosen! Blessed the guest at home in your place! We expect our fill of good things in your house, your heavenly manse. . . . Dawn and dusk take turns calling, "Come and worship."
Psalm 65:1–4, 8 msg

In the stillness of this moment, Lord, I come before You, in silent wonder of who You are, what You have done, and how You have worked in my life. Hear my prayer, Lord, as my lips praise You. Free me of the missteps, the mistakes I have made, the guilt that weighs me down. Lord, cleanse me of all shadows. Leave only Your light behind and within me. Here, in Your presence, I feel I am home. Thank You for opening Your door to me. For choosing me, saving me, and loving me. What joy I find within these cloud-formed walls in Your heavenly dwelling, my provider, my God. Here I find all I need. Here, at Your feet, I worship. In Jesus' name, amen.

Day 281

HE SEES YOU

Why do you say, Israel, "My way is hidden from the Lord;
my cause is disregarded by my God"? Do you not know?
Have you not heard? The Lord is the everlasting God,
the Creator of the ends of the earth. He will not grow tired
or weary, and his understanding no one can fathom.
ISAIAH 40:27–28

God, I'm struggling right now. I'm feeling vulnerable and invisible. My strength is waning, and I'm not sure I can go on like this. Do You see me? Look at this mess. Where is my help? I'm tired. Have You forgotten me here? No. I know that You haven't. My ways are not hidden from Your sight. You shield the weak and heavy-laden of Your flock, and You are gentle with me when I need special care. Open my eyes to the ways You are caring for me even now. You know my needs and give me just the right amount of strength to get through my difficulty. I am never alone. Your eye is always on me. Forgive me for complaining instead of trusting. Amen.

Day 282
THE HEAD—LIFTING GOD

We couldn't settle down. The fights in the church and the fears in our hearts kept us on pins and needles. We couldn't relax because we didn't know how it would turn out. Then the God who lifts up the downcast lifted our heads and our hearts with the arrival of Titus. We were glad just to see him, but the true reassurance came in. . .how much you cared, how much you grieved, how concerned you were for me. I went from worry to tranquility in no time!
2 Corinthians 7:5–7 MSG

So often battles are going on outside me while at the same time I'm fending off fears within me, Lord. Being so conflicted within and without makes it hard to be able to relax. And constantly worrying about how things will turn out in the end doesn't do much for my peace of mind and heart. But then You send someone or something my way—an encourager or a blessing— and suddenly I'm looking up once more. I'm remembering how much You care for me. And before I know it, frets fly out the window and peace stills my soul. Thank You, Lord, for being the lifter of my head and my heart. Amen.

Day 283

OVERFLOW WITH JOY

In all our affliction, I am overflowing with joy. For even
when we came into Macedonia, our bodies had no rest,
but we were afflicted at every turn—fighting without
and fear within. But God, who comforts the downcast,
comforted us by the coming of Titus, and not only by
his coming but also by the comfort with which he was
comforted by you. . .so that I rejoiced still more.
2 Corinthians 7:4–7 esv

It's amazing, Lord, how contagious our emotions can be! What I express has an effect on all those around me! So, help me, Lord, to overflow with joy—no matter what is going on in my life. To find and tap into that deep, abiding lode of spiritual joy You have waiting for me, streaming just beneath the surface. As You comfort me and fill me with gladness, my friends, family, coworkers, and even complete strangers will find themselves eased in their own pain and affliction. Our fighting without and fears within will dissipate and become as nothing but fool's gold, something that is easily thrown away as we treasure what we have in You! Amen!

Day 284
WHITER THAN SNOW

*O God, favor me because of Your loving-kindness.
Take away my wrong-doing because of the greatness
of Your loving-pity. . . . I have sinned against You, and
You only. . . . Take away my sin, and I will be clean. Wash
me, and I will be whiter than snow. Make me hear joy
and happiness. . . . Make a clean heart in me, O God.*
PSALM 51:1, 4, 7–8, 10 NLV

Lord, I have hurt someone. I have injured another person. And I'm filled with remorse, for not only have I harmed another, but I have disobeyed You in the process. Thus, I have sinned against You at the same time. Both bring me shame, Lord. But doing wrong to You truly hurts my heart. So I come to You on my knees. I ask You for forgiveness. For cleansing. For a new heart and a fresh start. Wash me within and without, Lord. Supply me with the words of apology to the person I have harmed. At the same time, Lord, help me forgive those who have hurt me. And before I leave this prayer, this place, this space, Lord, "make me hear joy and happiness" in You once more. Amen.

Day 285
PROMISE KEEPER

*"God is not human, that he should lie, not a human
being, that he should change his mind. Does he speak
and then not act? Does he promise and not fulfill?"*
NUMBERS 23:19

God, I'm ashamed to say that I've made empty promises before. Whether I fully intended to keep my word and then got distracted from my purpose or knew that I most likely wouldn't follow through, it's still a broken promise. I'm guilty of changing my mind, failing to act when I should, and forgetting at times. Unlike me, God, You always keep Your word and never change Your mind. Your promises are brimming with hope because I know that they aren't empty platitudes. The full weight of Your divine personality backs them up. You always do what You say You will. Where I have failed to meet the standard, You are the ultimate promise keeper. In the name of Jesus, amen.

Day 286
SWEET SLEEP

Keep sound and godly Wisdom and discretion, and they will be life to your inner self, and a gracious ornament to your neck (your outer self). Then you will walk in your way securely and in confident trust, and you shall not dash your foot or stumble. When you lie down, you shall not be afraid; yes, you shall lie down, and your sleep shall be sweet.
PROVERBS 3:21–24 AMPC

My day usually begins well, Lord, because I wake up with You in my mind and heart. But then, as my day goes on, I get distracted with the world. Before I know it, I'm doing, working, living, loving in *my* wisdom and strength, not Yours. That's when things start to fall apart. That's when I start to trip over my own thoughts and end up flat on my face. By the end of the day, I'm beaten and bruised, and sleep becomes elusive at best. So, help me regain my peace by keeping and following Your wisdom and ways all through my day. As I do, I know I'll find calm and sweet sleep in the secret place of Your presence. In Jesus' name, amen.

Day 287

HEAVENLY DEW

You will guard him and keep him in perfect and constant peace whose mind [both its inclination and its character] is stayed on You, because he commits himself to You, leans on You, and hopes confidently in You. So trust in the Lord (commit yourself to Him, lean on Him, hope confidently in Him) forever. . . . You who dwell in the dust, awake and sing for joy! For Your dew [O Lord] is a dew of [sparkling] light [heavenly, supernatural dew].
ISAIAH 26:3–4, 19 AMPC

I'm keeping my mind, heart, soul, and spirit focused on You, Lord. For when I do, Your guard of peace comes up all around me. Its shield keeps me still within, no matter what is happening without. In You I find my refuge, for to You alone I am committed. On You alone I lean. All my hope and expectation lie in You—not just today, in this moment on earth, but forever. Beyond this day and all the days to come. Rain down Your love upon me, Lord. For it's Your refreshment that keeps me from running dry and in the current of Your presence and all the love and joy that come with it. Amen.

Day 288

NIGHT HOURS

My lips will praise You because Your loving-kindness is better than life. . . . On my bed I remember You. I think of You through the hours of the night. For You have been my help. And I sing for joy in the shadow of Your wings. My soul holds on to You. Your right hand holds me up. . . . All who are faithful to God will be full of joy.
PSALM 63:3, 6–8, 11 NLV

Lord, there is no better or greater thing in my life than Your love for me and Your never-ending kindness to me. When I climb into bed at the end of the day, I think of You. I pray to You. I ask You for blessings, for compassion on me and those I love. And amid that nightly prayer to You, I fall not only asleep but into Your arms. Thank You for holding me, helping me, hiding me, and hovering over me. In You I find my rest, my shelter, my peace. I'm clinging to You, Lord, holding on tight. For You are my salvation. You are my joy. In You alone do I trust and find my way. Amen.

Day 289

UNSHAKABLE

*I keep my eyes always on the Lord. With him at my
right hand, I will not be shaken. Therefore my heart
is glad and my tongue rejoices. . . . You make known
to me the path of life; you will fill me with joy in your
presence, with eternal pleasures at your right hand.*
PSALM 16:8–9, 11

Lord, I love living in Your presence. When I wander from Your
side and become distracted by the offerings of this world, I lose
my peace and joy and my sense of purpose. I begin to wonder,
What's the point of all this struggle? But when my eyes are on
You, I am unshakable. Joy explodes within me, and my purpose
here is crystal clear. Without You, I have no reason. Without You,
nothing makes sense and life is meaningless. But with You, God,
I know that this world is but a prelude to my real life in eternity
with You. And oh, what joys and unimaginable pleasure I will experience when I meet You face-to-face. In Jesus' name, amen.

Day 290
SIT BACK AND RELAX

Ruth told her everything that the man had done for her, adding, "And he gave me all this barley besides—six quarts! He told me, 'You can't go back empty-handed to your mother-in-law!'" Naomi said, "Sit back and relax, my dear daughter, until we find out how things turn out; this man isn't going to waste any time. Mark my words, he's going to get everything wrapped up today."
RUTH 3:16–18 MSG

When I'm waiting to see how things are going to turn out, Lord, I don't just get anxious; I also get grouchy. Then before I know it, all kinds of scenarios begin playing out in my mind. And soon, any semblance of peace that remained within me has taken flight. So help me take the advice that Naomi gave to Ruth, Lord. Help me not to worry or freak out over imaginary scenarios that may never come to pass and instead "sit back and relax" until I see how things are going to turn out. Help me to leave all in Your hands, knowing You always know best. In Jesus' name, amen.

Day 291

EAGERLY AWAITING

*I bore you on eagles' wings and brought you to
Myself. . . . The eternal God is your refuge and dwelling
place, and underneath are the everlasting arms. . . . [Looking
forward to the shepherd's arrival, the eager girl pictures
their meeting and says]. . .Oh, that his left hand were under
my head and that his right hand embraced me! . . . Let all
those that seek and require You rejoice and be glad in You.*
EXODUS 19:4; DEUTERONOMY 33:27; SONG OF
SOLOMON 8:1, 3; PSALM 40:16 AMPC

Lord, thank You for hovering over me. For bearing me on eagles' wings, bringing me out of myself and into You. You are my refuge. In You I live, move, and have my being. You hold me up when I'm down. You turn my life around. Each and every morning, I look for You, eagerly anticipating the calm, peace, love, and joy I'll experience when Your left hand gently cradles my head and Your right hand draws me into You. Come, Lord, I'm waiting. I'm willing and ready to melt into Your love and affection. In Jesus' name I pray, amen.

Day 292
WONDER AND JOY

"Why are you troubled, and why do doubts arise in your hearts? See my hands and my feet, that it is I myself. Touch me, and see. For a spirit does not have flesh and bones as you see that I have." And when he had said this, he showed them his hands and his feet. And while they still disbelieved for joy and were marveling, he said to them, "Have you anything here to eat?"

LUKE 24:38–41 ESV

You amaze me, Lord. You show up, out of nowhere, whenever I need You. You tell me to calm down. Not to worry. Not to allow thoughts of doubt into my heart or mind. You point me to You, revealing all that You are and ever have been. You tell me the truth. That You are the Son of God, the one who died to save my soul. The one raised from the dead who lives to bring me to Father God. Some days, Lord, I cannot believe what You have done for me. I sit back amazed yet full of joy. Then You help me get on with the needs of the day, continually providing for me, leading me, guiding me. Oh Lord, You are my wonder and joy. Amen.

Day 293

REMEMBER ALL HIS BENEFITS

Praise the LORD, my soul, and forget not all his benefits—
who forgives all your sins and heals all your diseases, who
redeems your life from the pit and crowns you with love
and compassion, who satisfies your desires with good
things so that your youth is renewed like the eagle's.
PSALM 103:2–5

Lord, we celebrate Mother's Day to honor and appreciate our moms and Father's Day for our dads. We celebrate Memorial Day to remember our fallen veterans and soldiers, but how often do we celebrate just to remember all You have done for us? Do I dwell often enough on Your benefits? Lifting my depressed spirits should be as easy as remembering the numerous blessings You have bestowed on me and all Your people through the ages. I sit in church on Sunday and dwell on my anxiety and prioritize my to-do list when I should be remembering just how blessed You have made me. Help me make each Sunday and every day in between a day of remembrance, a day of counting blessings. In Jesus' name, amen.

Day 294
YOUR CONFIDENCE

*Be not afraid of sudden terror and panic, nor of the
stormy blast or the storm and ruin of the wicked when
it comes [for you will be guiltless], for the Lord shall be
your confidence, firm and strong, and shall keep your foot
from being caught [in a trap or some hidden danger].*
PROVERBS 3:25–26 AMPC

There's no peace for me, Lord, when I allow my imagination to run wild. When I hear of a danger, something bad that may or may not happen, the next thing I know, my mind is filled with a dozen different scenarios, none of them good. And I begin to accept those scenarios as reality when they are anything but! So I need Your help, Lord, to calm my racing heart, rein in my imagination, allay my fears, and lift this darkness hanging over me. I need You, Lord, to be my confidence. Help me to stand firm in You and Your Word when whorls of worries try to overtake me and panic pounces on me. Shine Your light on the recesses of my mind until all shadows dissipate and Your peace fills me once more. In Jesus' name, amen.

Day 295
A JOYFUL WALK WITH JESUS

*I am going. . .bound by the [Holy] Spirit and obligated
and compelled by the [convictions of my own] spirit, not
knowing what will befall me. . .except that the Holy Spirit
clearly and emphatically affirms to me. . .that imprisonment
and suffering await me. But none of these things move me;
neither do I esteem my life dear to myself, if only I may finish
my course with joy and the ministry which I have obtained
from [which was entrusted to me by] the Lord Jesus.*
ACTS 20:22–24 AMPC

I'm not really sure what lies before me, Lord. Only You can see
all things that have been, are, and will be. But I know that Your
Spirit is leading my spirit, urging me to move ahead, to continue
on with the gifts You have given me, in the direction You have
sent me. Whatever happens, good or bad, doesn't really matter
to me. The only desire I have is to finish my walk with You with
joy, working where and when You allow. Thank You, Lord, for
making me a part of Your plan. In Jesus' name, I pray, amen.

Day 296
A WILLING SPIRIT

Make a clean heart in me, O God. Give me a new spirit that will not be moved. Do not throw me away from where You are. And do not take Your Holy Spirit from me. Let the joy of Your saving power return to me. And give me a willing spirit to obey you. . . . Then my tongue will sing with joy about how right and good You are.
PSALM 51:10–12, 14 NLV

I've fallen short, Lord. I've misstepped. And so here I am before You, asking for forgiveness. For my sins to be washed away. For a clean heart—and a new spirit. One that will be stronger, not so easily led into sin, not so easily lured into temptation. Draw me near to You, Lord. I want to snuggle up close, to feel Your breath, to join my spirit with Yours. Return to me the joy of Your saving power, and make my spirit willingly obey You. I know my true joy and path lie in Your ways, not my own. Set me straight, Lord. Prepare me and my path as I joyfully praise You. Amen.

Day 297
HEART'S DESIRE

Don't worry about the wicked or envy those who do wrong.
For like grass, they soon fade away. Like spring flowers,
they soon wither. Trust in the LORD and do good. Then
you will live safely in the land and prosper. Take delight
in the LORD, and he will give you your heart's desires.
PSALM 37:1–4 NLT

Father, I can trust in Your provision because You always have my best interests at heart, even when I, at times, like a young child naive to potential harm, want things that aren't good for me. Those who live for themselves instead of You sometimes seem to be flourishing while I struggle to follow You. But all I have to do is look to my eternal future to find encouragement. My daffodils are glorious in early May, but their reign of beauty in my garden is fleeting. Soon their petals turn brown and crumble. The wicked will wither and fade like spring flowers. I will trust You and follow You, and You will fulfill all of my deepest longings. In Jesus' name, amen.

Day 298
STEPPING OUT

Peter, suddenly bold, said, "Master, if it's really you, call me to come to you on the water." He said, "Come ahead." Jumping out of the boat, Peter walked on the water to Jesus. But when he looked down at the waves churning beneath his feet, he lost his nerve and started to sink. He cried, "Master, save me!"
MATTHEW 14:28–30 MSG

There are moments, Jesus, when I have courage and am more than ready for the challenges before me. So I take a bold step forward, knowing that You, Master, have invited me to step out in faith. Eagerly, I take the leap. My feet wet, I walk out to You standing there, waiting for me. But then my focus veers away. My eyes see the waves roiling beneath me. I feel the wind spraying salt water on my face. My vision starts to blur, and the next thing I know, I'm sinking in fear. I cry out for You to save me. And that's what I'm doing right now in this moment, Lord— asking You to give me the strength to turn from my fears and walk forward in faith. Give me the power and peace I need to stay focused on You and You alone. Amen.

Day 299

OPEN TO JOY

Give strength to weak hands and to weak knees.
Say to those whose heart is afraid, "Have strength of
heart, and do not be afraid. See, your God will come. . . .
He will save you." Then the eyes of the blind will be opened.
And the ears of those who cannot hear will be opened.
Then those who cannot walk will jump like a deer. And the
tongue of those who cannot speak will call out for joy.
ISAIAH 35:3–6 NLV

Your Word, Lord—oh, how it feeds every part of me! It gives strength, power, and energy to my weak hands and knees. Your Word swells my heart, filling it with the courage I need to face things I'd rather not face, things I can overcome only when You stand with me. Your Word opens the eyes of my heart each time I look within its pages. Your voice reveals new meanings, helping me to understand things that were once cloudy. You make me want to leap and shout for joy! Continue with me, Lord. Today reveal the wonder and power of Your Word until my soul once again rejoices. Amen.

THE BOUNTIFUL EARTH

*You visit the earth and water it; you greatly enrich it;
the river of God is full of water; you provide their
grain. . . . You water its furrows abundantly, settling its
ridges, softening it with showers, and blessing its growth.
You crown the year with your bounty. . . . The pastures of
the wilderness overflow, the hills gird themselves with joy,
the meadows clothe themselves with flocks, the valleys deck
themselves with grain, they shout and sing together for joy.*
PSALM 65:9–13 ESV

I thank You, Lord, for the gift of this earth. For Your tender care of it and Your never-ending love for it. Give me that same love of the earth, Lord. Help me to be a better caretaker, to do what You would have me do to keep its waters flowing, its animals bountiful, its hills, plains, and meadows alive, joyful, and productive. You are not just the God of creation but also the Lord of abundance. As You provide for the earth, the earth, in turn, provides for me and mine. Help me to remember that, Lord. To thank You for this good earth that sings joyfully together with me in praise of You. Amen.

Day 301

STILL YOURS

*My heart was bitter, and I was all torn up inside. I was
so foolish and ignorant. . . . Yet I still belong to you;
you hold my right hand. You guide me with your counsel,
leading me to a glorious destiny. Whom have I in heaven
but you? I desire you more than anything on earth.
My health may fail, and my spirit may grow weak, but God
remains the strength of my heart; he is mine forever.*
PSALM 73:21–26 NLT

God, I'm so glad that even after I've been a fool, after I've envied the accomplishments and wealth and seeming ease of
those who don't follow You, I still belong to You. Show me how
much more You have waiting for me in the glorious eternity
You're preparing than the shallow and unfulfilling treasures of
this world. When I spend time with You and read Your scriptures,
I see things more clearly. Those who don't love You may prosper for a short time, but ultimately they will fall into ruin. Make
the prayer of my heart always be that I would desire You more
than anything I find here on earth. You are all I need. In Jesus'
name, amen.

Day 302
RETURN TO YOUR REST

The Lord is gracious and righteous; our God is compassionate. The Lord guards the inexperienced; I was helpless, and He saved me. Return to your rest, my soul, for the Lord has been good to you. For You, Lord, rescued me from death, my eyes from tears, my feet from stumbling. I will walk before the Lord in the land of the living.
PSALM 116:5–9 HCSB

When I lose my cool, Lord, I feel so helpless. And following hard on the heels of those feelings of helplessness are feelings of hopelessness. Experiencing those emotions makes me feel like I'm still a babe in Christ. I have so much growing up to do, it's almost embarrassing. And that steals even more of my peace. Yet I know You, my protector. You're full of compassion and empathy. When I'm helpless, You reach out and rescue me from death, tears, and stumbles. You are the one who keeps me on my feet. It is through Your love for me, Lord, that my heart finds peace and my soul finds rest. In Jesus' name, amen.

Day 303
GIVING FIRST TO GOD

[The Macedonian churches] have been put to the test by much trouble, but they have much joy. They have given much even though they were very poor. They gave as much as they could because they wanted to. They asked from their hearts if they could help the Christians in Jerusalem. It was more than we expected. They gave themselves to the Lord first. Then they gave themselves to us to be used as the Lord wanted.

2 CORINTHIANS 8:2–5 NLV

There is such joy in giving, Lord. But there are so many worthy causes. It can be difficult to know which to choose. So, Lord, make Your desires clear to me. As I give myself first to You, I'm relying on You to help me to home in on the causes You want me to support through service, provisions, or money. Lord, I want to give from the heart and soul. And after I do, I'm not going to worry about where my next dollar will be coming from but will rely on You to provide for me as I help provide for others—with absolute joy and pleasure. In Jesus' name, amen.

Day 304
GENUINE JOY

*Unlike the culture around you, always dragging you
down to its level of immaturity, God brings the best
out of you, develops well-formed maturity in you. . . .
If you're called to give aid to people in distress, keep
your eyes open and be quick to respond; if you work with
the disadvantaged, don't let yourself get irritated with
them or depressed by them. Keep a smile on your face.
Love from the center of who you are; don't fake it.*
ROMANS 12:2, 8–9 MSG

Help me, Lord Jesus, to be different from the culture around
me. Lift me up to You, lest I be dragged down into the chaos
of this world. Bring out the best in me so that I can be a useful
part of Your body. Open my eyes to people whom You want me
to help. Give me the resources to lift them as You have lifted
me. Keep me from getting irritated by those who are weak, suffering, disadvantaged, poor, or depressed. Help me to keep my
mind, heart, and ears open. Make me a good listener, free of
judgment. And above all, give me such deep joy that no matter
who I am helping, my smile toward them is genuine, an offshoot
of my happiness in and with You. Amen.

Day 305
SAFE IN HIS HAND

*"But ask the animals, and they will teach you, or the
birds in the sky, and they will tell you; or speak to the
earth, and it will teach you, or let the fish in the sea
inform you. Which of all these does not know that the
hand of the LORD has done this? In his hand is the life
of every creature and the breath of all mankind."*

JOB 12:7–10

Father, at times my life seems so small and fragile in this world
of unpredictability and scary circumstances. Who can say what
will happen in the next moment? But I can put my anxiety at
ease because I rest in Your hand. I am vulnerable and weak,
but nothing can take me out of Your palm. That doesn't mean
that hard things will never come to me, but I know that when
they do, You will be there with me. You will lend me Your strength
and make sure I have everything I need to come through my tri-
als in Your power. When I am weak, You are strong. Your power
works most effectively in my weakness. I am held and comforted by You. Amen.

Day 306

THE BIG HELP

I will lift up my eyes to the mountains. Where will my help come from? My help comes from the Lord, Who made heaven and earth. He will not let your feet go out from under you. He Who watches over you will not sleep. Listen, He Who watches over Israel will not close his eyes or sleep.
PSALM 121:1–4 NLV

Walking along the road of life, Lord, I often discover that my focus is more on where I'll land than on where I actually am. But You have advised me, Lord, to live in the present, not the future. So today I lift my eyes up to You, Your mountains, Your heights. For You, the Creator and caretaker of all, are all the help I need. You will not let me trip up. You're the one who watches over me when I sleep. In fact, You, my defender, never close Your eyes. Be my lookout, my ever-vigilant protector. Keep me from losing my way, from losing my courage, from losing my peace. Lord, You are the one who holds me and mine in Your hands forevermore. Amen.

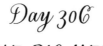

Day 307
A JOYFUL COMEBACK

"Come back to me and really mean it!" . . . Change your life, not just your clothes. Come back to God, your God. And here's why: God is kind and merciful. He takes a deep breath, puts up with a lot, this most patient God, extravagant in love, always ready to cancel catastrophe. Who knows? Maybe he'll do it now, maybe he'll turn around and show pity. Maybe, when all's said and done, there'll be blessings full and robust for your God!
JOEL 2:12–14 MSG

Lord, I know sometimes I'm just not there for You. Not like You're always here for me. I've gotten so busy living life, I've forgotten to live it for You! As a result, all joy seems to have gone out of me. So forgive me, God, for wandering away. I know You are kind, loving, and compassionate. You have so much more love for me than I do for myself right now, Lord. So let's change things up. As I come back to You, Lord, come back to me. Turn my life around to the good. Shower Your blessings upon me as I joyfully await Your power and presence in my life once more! In Jesus' name, amen.

Day 308
PRESENT JOY

[The once-exiled and now-returned Israelites] sang, praising and giving thanks to the Lord, saying, "For He is good, for His loving-kindness is upon Israel forever." All the people called out with a loud voice when they praised the Lord because the work on the house of the Lord had begun. But many. . .had seen the first house of the Lord. And they cried with a loud voice. . . . But many called out for joy in a loud voice.
EZRA 3:11–12 NLV

Sometimes, Lord, I can really mess up a good thing. Then when I try to rebuild, the new doesn't seem like it will be better than— or even as good as—what was there before. Either way, Lord, help me to have hope. To rejoice at whatever new thing You are doing. Although it may be okay to spend a little time grieving over the loss of what once was, don't let me stay there. Give me the courage to look away from the past and into the present. Help me to praise what You are doing now. To see the new thing You have prepared. To remember how good You have been, are now, and always will be. Wrap me in Your present joy. In Jesus' name, amen.

Day 309
REMARKABLE SECRETS

"This is what the Lord says—the Lord who made the earth, who formed and established it, whose name is the Lord: Ask me and I will tell you remarkable secrets you do not know about things to come."
JEREMIAH 33:2–3 NLT

God, I see people around me chasing after fleeting pleasures and finding empty satisfaction in the comforts of this world. They ignore You and Your plan and think that this life is a race to have as much fun as they can before they die. But since I've come to know You, it's as if You've shared a secret with me. You've shown me what living really means and given me a sneak peek into the marvelous things You have in store for me both now and when I pass through the veil into eternity. Knowing even just a hint of Your amazing plan strengthens my faith and my decision to follow Your ways. Tell me more of Your secrets, God. In the name of Jesus, amen.

Day 310

FAN THE FLAMES OF LOVE

Get along among yourselves, each of you doing your part. . . . Gently encourage the stragglers, and reach out for the exhausted. . . . Be patient with each person, attentive to individual needs. . . . Don't snap at each other. Look for the best in each other, and always do your best to bring it out. Be cheerful no matter what; pray all the time; thank God no matter what happens. This is the way God wants you who belong to Christ Jesus to live.
1 Thessalonians 5:13–18 msg

One way to maintain my peace, within and without, Lord, is to be like Jesus. But for that, I'll definitely need Your unerring wisdom and supernatural assistance. Help me, Lord, to do that work You've put in my hands to do. Give me words of encouragement to share with people who are exhausted as well as the patience to persevere, allowing people to find their way at their own pace. Most of all, Lord, help me to look for the best in others, not the worst. Help me to find Your light within each human being. Then, Lord, give me the words that will fan their flames of love. In Jesus' name I serve and pray. Amen.

Day 311
FREEDOM TO CHOOSE

*You were chosen to be free. Be careful that you do
not please your old selves by sinning because you are
free. Live this free life by loving and helping others. . . .
Let the Holy Spirit lead you in each step. Then you will
not please your sinful old selves. . . . The fruit that comes
from having the Holy Spirit in our lives is: love, joy, peace,
not giving up, being kind, being good, having faith,
being gentle, and being the boss over our own desires.*
GALATIANS 5:13, 16, 22–23 NLV

Your Word, Lord, makes it clear that You *chose* me to be free!
For that privilege, I praise You, Lord. Yet I don't want that same
freedom to lead me to please myself. I want to please *You*. And
the only way to do that is by letting Your Holy Spirit lead me
every way, every day. So, help me, Lord, to keep close to You.
To home in on what the Holy Spirit would have me do, where
He would have me go. Then I will have the love, joy, peace, and
so much more that comes from walking in Your will and way! In
Jesus' name, I pray, amen.

Day 312

THE TRUE SOURCE

"You heard the words that I said, 'I am not the Christ, but I have been sent before Him.' The man who has just been married has the bride. The friend of the man just married stands at his side and listens to him. He has joy when he hears the voice of the man just married. I am full of this joy. He must become more important. I must become less important."
JOHN 3:28–30 NLV

Jesus, nothing gives me more joy than when I bring You to the attention of a nonbeliever—and then that nonbeliever begins to experience You, follow You, love and worship You as I do. But afterward, Lord, help me to slip away to the sidelines. To get out of the way of Your light. Help me to be humble enough to let the newly born in You know *You* are the source of both our joy. That You are the true path, the real way, and I am just a signpost along the road. For You alone are the one and only Son. The one who plants and nourishes the joy in our lives and love in our hearts. In Your name, I pray, amen.

Day 343
GOD'S YES!

No matter how many promises God has made, they are
"Yes" in Christ. And so through him the "Amen" is spoken
by us to the glory of God. Now it is God who makes
both us and you stand firm in Christ. He anointed us,
set his seal of ownership on us, and put his Spirit in our
hearts as a deposit, guaranteeing what is to come.
2 CORINTHIANS 1:20–22

God, I'm so accustomed to hearing the disappointing word *no*.
I even say it all the time to my children: "No, no, no, you may
not do that or have that." But Your answer to me through Jesus
is yes! Yes, I am a daughter in Christ. Yes, I can stand firm and
leave my life of sin. Yes, I do have new life. Yes, I can have joy.
Yes, I am empowered by Your Spirit and sealed as Yours. Yes, I
will inherit eternal life. Your Holy Spirit is our guarantee that all
Your promises will come true. Not a word You have uttered will
be left unfulfilled. Thank You, God, for Your yes! In the name of
Jesus, amen.

Day 314
HEART SET

"If you set your heart on God and reach out to him, if you scrub your hands of sin and refuse to entertain evil in your home. . . . You'll forget your troubles. . . . Your world will be washed in sunshine, every shadow dispersed by dawn. Full of hope, you'll relax, confident again; you'll look around, sit back, and take it easy. Expansive, without a care in the world, you'll be hunted out by many for your blessing."
JOB 11:13–14, 16–19 MSG

My troubles have been weighing me down, Lord, keeping me anxious, afraid, distracted. I'm so full of worry that I'm neither walking forward or backward. I'm stuck in this one spot. I need hope, Lord—hope that things will get better. That someday all my confusion, woes, and fears will drop away. That peace will then follow. For now, Lord, I'm going to do what I can from my end. I'm setting my heart on and reaching out to You, embracing good and eschewing evil. For when I do, Your Word tells me my troubles will soon be forgotten, as if they never were. As hope will once more reign, I'll be able to relax, take it easy, in You. Amen.

Day 315
REGAINING STRENGTH

Let them give Him gifts of thanks and tell of His works with songs of joy. Some went out to sea in ships. . . . He spoke and raised up a storm. . . . Their strength of heart left them in their danger. . . . They did not know what to do. Then they cried out to the Lord in their trouble. And He took them out of all their problems. He stopped the storm, and the waves of the sea became quiet. Then they were glad because the sea became quiet. And He led them to the safe place they wanted.
PSALM 107:22–23, 25–30 NLV

When I go out on my own, I usually end up exhausted, just when I need the most strength. That's when I finally realize I've left You out of my boat, Lord. I cry to You, and You come to my rescue. You stop the wind and the waves. In the quiet, I hear Your voice. I'm overwhelmed with gladness. My heart regains strength. And You lead me to the exact place I'd been heading all along. Thank You, Lord, for always being there for me, helping me, rescuing me, delivering me. Amen.

Day 316
OPEN WIDE

Sing aloud to God our Strength! Shout for joy. . . .
You called in distress and I delivered you; I answered
you in the secret place of thunder; I tested you at the
waters of Meribah. . . . I am the Lord your God, Who
brought you up out of the land of Egypt. Open your
mouth wide and I will fill it. . . . Oh, that My people
would listen to Me, that Israel would walk in My ways!
PSALM 81:1, 7, 10, 13 AMPC

From You, Lord, I get the strength to overcome. To You, I shout for joy. Whenever I call, Lord, You answer. When I am in need, You provide an answer. You are the one who continually rescues me. You part the sea so I can flee my foes. You subdue rulers so I can find my way to freedom in You. When I am hungry, You fill my mouth with food. When I am thirsty, You provide water from a rock. My joy lies in following You, obeying You, listening to You. For only when I walk in Your way am I on the right road to joy and Your kingdom. Amen.

Day 317
STAY WITH GOD

*I'm sure now I'll see God's goodness in the
exuberant earth. Stay with GOD! Take heart.
Don't quit. I'll say it again: Stay with GOD.*
PSALM 27:13–14 MSG

God, I'm going to stick with You through this winding trek of
life. I'm not going to quit even when I don't understand what
You're doing. I'm going to trust. I'm going to wait for You. I see
Your goodness all around me. It's evident in the crimson fingers
streaking the dawn sky. It dances with the laughter of a child. It
pours out with the quenching spring rain and the bright blos-
soms of May flowers. I see it in a stranger's smile. I feel it in
the love I have for my family. You are a good Father. I will keep
eternity in sight as my motivation to keep living for You, to keep
doing the right thing until the end of my days here. Amen.

Day 318
BUILD UP

Every wise woman builds her house, but a foolish one tears it down with her own hands. . . . The heart knows its own bitterness, and no outsider shares in its joy. . . . A wise man is cautious and turns from evil, but a fool is easily angered and is careless. . . . A tranquil heart is life to the body, but jealousy is rottenness to the bones.
PROVERBS 14:1, 10, 16, 30 HCSB

There are times, Lord, when I hear myself speak and find myself wincing in pain. For the words that can sometimes fly out of my mouth are harmful ones, words I'm not proud of. They seem to end up tearing others down instead of building them up. Perhaps there's some bitterness and unforgiveness I need to deal with. But in the meantime, Lord, remind me to think before I speak. Help me not to lose my temper but to make it my aim to hold nothing but peace and love in my heart. For then the words that come from my mouth will help, not hinder, their hearers, including me. Amen.

Day 319
THIRSTING FOR GOD'S VOICE

*Wait and listen, everyone who is thirsty! Come to the waters;
and he who has no money, come, buy and eat! Yes, come,
buy [priceless, spiritual] wine and milk without money and
without price [simply for the self-surrender that accepts
the blessing]. Why do you spend your money for that which
is not bread, and your earnings for what does not satisfy?
Hearken diligently to Me, and eat what is good, and let your
soul delight itself in fatness [the profuseness of spiritual joy].*
ISAIAH 55:1–2 AMPC

Lord, I am so ready to drink from Your well of wisdom. There are
so many voices out there, telling me what is right and what is
wrong, what I should do and what I shouldn't do. Help me, Lord,
silence the words—written and spoken—of others that are ring-
ing through my head. Give me the power and strength to focus
on Yours alone. What You have within Your Book is the wisdom
I crave. Show me what You would have me read. Then open the
doors of my mind so that I can comprehend what You're telling
me. Give my soul the joy and delight of Your direction! In Jesus'
name, I pray, amen.

Day 320
A SPECIAL PLACE

Do not let your hearts be troubled (distressed, agitated).
You believe in and adhere to and trust in and rely on
God; believe in and adhere to and trust in and rely
also on Me. In My Father's house there are many
dwelling places (homes). If it were not so, I would have
told you; for I am going away to prepare a place for
you. . . . Where I am going, you know the way.
JOHN 14:1–2, 4 AMPC

Some days the woes, worries, and what-ifs come tumbling upon me, Lord. I get weighted down by this world so easily. And then I remember Your words. You've told me not to let my heart and mind be troubled but to trust in You, to lean on and rely on God. You've made it clear that You have a place for me in Father God's house. A room that You have prepared—just for me! I know the way there, so I'm running to You, Lord. Lift me up to that room, the one where I'll find You. That secret place of joy, where all my troubles melt away as I melt into You. Amen.

Day 321

PRECIOUS TO HIM

Long ago the LORD said to Israel: "I have loved you, my people, with an everlasting love. With unfailing love I have drawn you to myself. I will rebuild you, my virgin Israel. You will again be happy and dance merrily with your tambourines."
JEREMIAH 31:3–4 NLT

Father, show me how You see me. I have allowed negative thought processes and self-criticism to distort Your opinion of me. Sometimes when I picture Your face, it's frowning in judgment. I know the enemy is putting lies in my head, because Your Word says there's no condemnation for Your children. And I am Your precious daughter. You love me with an everlasting love and have drawn me to You. You are pleased with me, Father, delighted to have me as Your child. You want happiness and goodness for my life, not suffering and turmoil. Reveal the lies I've been believing about You, and teach me the truth You want me to know about Your unfailing love for me. In the name of Jesus, amen.

Day 322
WAITING IN SILENCE

*For God alone my soul waits in silence; from Him comes
my salvation. He only is my Rock and my Salvation,
my Defense and my Fortress, I shall not be greatly
moved. . . . My soul, wait only upon God and silently
submit to Him; for my hope and expectation are from
Him. He only is my Rock and my Salvation; He is my
Defense and my Fortress, I shall not be moved.*
PSALM 62:1–2, 5–6 AMPC

My patience, Lord, is wearing thin. That means that hour by
hour, day by day, my peace has been leaking away. Now it's almost gone. And that will not do. So I come to You today, Lord.
My soul waits silently before You, my Rock and my Savior. Here
in Your presence I can rest. Here I will sit until You speak. For I
know that it is in the deep, deep silence that I will clearly hear
Your voice, Your direction, Your wisdom, Your answer. You alone
can tell me when You are ready for me to move. And until then,
I wait in expectancy and hope. In You, my supreme fortress, defense, and peace. In Jesus' name I live and pray. Amen.

Day 323
ROOTS IN REALITY

Every time you cross my mind, I break out in exclamations of thanks to God. Each exclamation is a trigger to prayer. I find myself praying for you with a glad heart. . . . There has never been the slightest doubt in my mind that the God who started this great work in you would keep at it and bring it to a flourishing finish. . . . It's not at all fanciful for me to think this way about you. My prayers and hopes have deep roots in reality.
PHILIPPIANS 1:3–4, 6–7 MSG

So many "things" go through my mind in one day, one hour, one moment, one second, Lord. And sometimes I never stop to dwell on any of them. I just keep focused on the task before me. Yet in doing that, Lord, I can miss Your prompts to pray for someone. So, Lord, help me break out in joyful recognition when someone crosses my mind. Allow that face or name to trigger a prayer on his or her behalf. May I pray that whatever You've begun in that individual will flourish. For prayers aren't just empty incantations—they change reality! In Jesus' name, amen!

Day 324
HOW BEAUTIFUL

How beautiful are the places where You live, O Lord of all!
My soul wants and even becomes weak from wanting to
be in the house of the Lord. My heart and my flesh sing for
joy to the living God. Even the bird has found a home. The
swallow has found a nest for herself where she may lay her
young at Your altars, O Lord of all, my King and my God.
PSALM 84:1–3 NLV

Where You live, Lord, must be amazing. I cannot even wrap my mind around what it might look like. Greater than the Taj Mahal. More amazing than the Grand Canyon. More beautiful than a Caribbean island. Wherever You are, in heaven or on earth, my soul longs to meet You, to be with You. There's no place I desire to be more than where You are. For You accept the humblest and simplest of creatures. When I, Your daughter, come to You, I feel like a princess in a palace. In You, my Father and King, is where I find my real home, where love, warmth, joy, and wonder rise up to greet me. As I follow Your light, I enter in, oh Lord, and bow at Your throne. Amen.

Day 325
PURE PROMISES

*Into the hovels of the poor, into the dark streets where
the homeless groan, God speaks: "I've had enough;
I'm on my way to heal the ache in the heart of the
wretched." God's words are pure words, pure silver words
refined seven times in the fires of his word-kiln, pure
on earth as well as in heaven. GOD, keep us safe from
their lies, from the wicked who stalk us with lies.*
PSALM 12:5–7 MSG

God, You speak into our messes. In the dark hovels where we hide and suffer, Your words penetrate the gloom and desperation to bring light and life. You came to heal our wretched hearts. To soothe away the ache in our lives and replace it with hope in You—hope in Your promises to care for us and give us a good future. You have plans for me. Plans that have nothing to do with disaster and depression. Instead You orchestrate hope and goodness into my future with You. Help me to hold tightly to Your promises amid the world's lies, because Your words are flawless, like silver refined in a crucible. It's not in Your nature to speak an untrue word. In Jesus' name, amen.

Day 326
BEGINNING NOW

With God rests my salvation and my glory; He is my Rock of unyielding strength and impenetrable hardness, and my refuge is in God! Trust in, lean on, rely on, and have confidence in Him at all times, you people; pour out your hearts before Him. God is a refuge for us (a fortress and a high tower). Selah [pause, and calmly think of that]!
PSALM 62:7–8 AMPC

I have so many things on my mind, Lord, and they're sapping me of my strength for each one carries with it a potential concern. Yet since concerns are what I'm *not* to be focused on, I've been trying to tamp down all my worries. Unfortunately, today I feel like all my frets have imploded within me, knocking me off balance. So I'm running to You, Lord, my high tower. I'm pouring out to You all the worries that have been building up inside me, stealing my peace, darkening my heart. One by one, I leave my woes at Your feet, beginning right now, in this moment. Amen.

Day 327
MIND EXCHANGE

Incline your ear [submit and consent to the divine will] and come to Me; hear, and your soul will revive. . . . Seek, inquire for, and require the Lord while He may be found [claiming Him by necessity and by right]; call upon Him while He is near. . . . For My thoughts are not your thoughts, neither are your ways My ways, says the Lord. . . . You shall go out. . .with joy and be led forth [by your Leader, the Lord Himself, and His word] with peace.
ISAIAH 55:3, 6, 8, 12 AMPC

Help me to readjust my ears so that I can pick up on Your wavelength, Lord. I'm drawing near to You, waiting and wanting to hear what You have to say. Refresh my soul, Lord, with Your Word as I seek Your face while You're so near to me. I'm calling out to You, emptying my own mind of its constant dialogue so that I can actually *hear* Your voice and exchange my thoughts for Yours, which are always so far above me yet penetrate deep into my own heart. For when I tap into Your wisdom and love, I find myself tasting Your joy and being led, not just by Your peace but by You Yourself! Amen.

Day 328
GENTLE STRENGTH

How happy are those who live in Your house! They are always giving thanks to You. How happy is the man whose strength is in You and in whose heart are the roads to Zion! As they pass through the dry valley of Baca, they make it a place of good water. The early rain fills the pools with good also. They go from strength to strength. Every one of them stands before God.
PSALM 84:4–7 NLV

The more time I spend with You, Jesus—studying Your Word, praying Your way, absorbing Your truths, following Your will—the stronger I seem to become. At each point, at each trial, I learn more, grow more, and find myself closer and closer to You. Yet while my strength is increasing, I have become gentler and find more peace, even in the midst of trial. All this gives me such joy. The unshakable kind. The joy that makes my foundation in You so firm. Thank You, Lord, for being everywhere I look. Everywhere I love. Everywhere I roam, from strength to strength, I'm home in You. Amen.

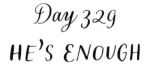

Day 329
HE'S ENOUGH

Jesus Christ is the same yesterday and today and forever.
Do not be carried away by all kinds of strange teachings.
It is good for our hearts to be strengthened by grace.
HEBREWS 13:8–9

Father, some think that Your plan is too easy—just ask and receive. They want to add more and require some further action on our part. Surely, we should have to clean ourselves up a bit and try to be presentable. But they've missed the truth that we need You so desperately because we're helpless to rescue ourselves. We can't add anything to the beautiful simplicity of Your grace. Jesus was enough then, and He's enough now. His sacrifice was sufficient for my sin—all of it. I can never go so far that Your grace won't cover me. And that will never change because You never change. Strengthen my heart with Your amazing, boundless, wonderful, and completely undeserved grace. In Jesus' name, amen.

Day 330
COMING AND GOING

The Lord watches over you. The Lord is your safe cover at your right hand. The sun will not hurt you during the day and the moon will not hurt you during the night. The Lord will keep you from all that is sinful. He will watch over your soul. The Lord will watch over your coming and going, now and forever.
PSALM 121:5–8 NLV

I love the idea of You watching over me, Lord, covering me from all dangers within and without. Because of You and Your 24-7 vigilance, I need not worry about being harmed during the day or when I sleep at night. You are a massive shield of protection that surrounds me—no matter where I am or who I am with or what I am doing. I need no special tool, phone, book, computer, or electronic device to call You or reach You. No, I have a direct line to You through prayer. So help me keep that in mind, Lord, as I go through my day. May the idea that You are watching me now and will do so forever help me not only keep my peace but revel in it, for You are the source of calm I yearn for. In Jesus' name, amen.

Day 331
HAPPY IN FAITH

Because of your prayers and the help the Holy Spirit gives me, all of this will turn out for good. . . . To me, living means having Christ. To die means that I would have more of Him. If I keep on living here in this body, it means that I can lead more people to Christ. . . . I have a desire to leave this world to be with Christ, which is much better. But it is more important for you that I stay. I am sure I will live to help you grow and be happy in your faith.
PHILIPPIANS 1:19, 21–25 NLV

Some days, Lord, life can be so hard that I just want You to beam me up. To lift up every part of me into heaven with You. Yet I know You have plans for me that are for my good and Your purpose. So help me to be happy wherever I am, Lord, in heaven or on earth. Remind me that things will, in the end, always turn out for good. Show me, Lord, whom You would have me help and whom You would have me lead to You so they can find joy in You. I live to serve You, Lord. In Jesus' name. Amen.

Day 332
LORD KNOWS

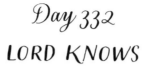

The heart knows its own bitterness, and no stranger shares its joy. . . . In the reverent and worshipful fear of the Lord there is strong confidence, and His children shall always have a place of refuge. . . . A calm and undisturbed mind and heart are the life and health of the body. . . . Wisdom rests [silently] in the mind and heart of him who has understanding.
PROVERBS 14:10, 26, 30, 33 AMPC

Only You can fully understand and empathize with the sorrow I bear in my heart, Lord. And yet at the same time, only You can fully understand, know, and take part in the joy I experience as well. Whether joyful or sad, I know You are with me, tending me, caring for me, crying or laughing with me. In You I find shelter from the storms of life. You give me the peace I crave. You calm my heart, quiet my spirit. Give me the wisdom, Lord, to run to You whether I am in tears or rolling with laughter. Share my life, sorrows, and joys, Lord, as I live and move in You. Amen.

Day 333
EVEN IF. . .

Shadrach, Meshach, and Abednego replied, "O Nebuchadnezzar, we do not need to defend ourselves before you. If we are thrown into the blazing furnace, the God whom we serve is able to save us. He will rescue us from your power, Your Majesty. But even if he doesn't, we want to make it clear to you, Your Majesty, that we will never serve your gods or worship the gold statue you have set up."
DANIEL 3:16–18 NLT

God, Your ways are so much bigger than me. And yet You care about my experiences. You see every hurt and capture my tears in a bottle. You see every slight, every unkind word said to me, every unfair action against me, and You take note. You know me intimately and love me greater than anyone else loves me. I trust that You are able to redeem the harm that others intend for me and use it for Your glory. You are powerful enough to deliver me from whatever blazing furnace I find myself in, but I know that even if You don't, there's more than this life waiting for me on the other side. Show me the breathtaking maturity You envision for me out of the ashes of my struggles. Amen.

Day 334
BREAKING THROUGH

David asked the Lord, "Should I go up against the Philistines? Will You give them into my hand?" And the Lord said to David, "Go up, for it is sure that I will give the Philistines into your hand." So David came to Baal-perazim and beat them there in battle. He said, "The Lord has broken through those who hate me like the breaking through of a flood."
2 SAMUEL 5:19–20 NLV

When people, situations, and things come against me, Lord, I find myself either cowering in the corner, speed walking the other way, or physically lashing out in some way—all before coming to You and asking for Your advice or help. Then, before I know it, everything, including me, starts breaking apart, and I'm not just down for the count, but I've lost whatever fragile peace I started out with, putting me in even more trouble than before. This time I'm asking You, Lord, what to do, knowing that with You on my side, nothing can defeat me or disturb my calm in You. For You break through all barriers. You protect me from all that comes against me. You, Lord, *are* my breakthrough. Amen.

Day 335
THAT MIDDLE GROUND

If any person thinks himself to be somebody [too important to condescend to shoulder another's load] when he is nobody [of superiority except in his own estimation], he deceives and deludes and cheats himself. But let every person carefully scrutinize and examine and test his own conduct and his own work. He can then have the personal satisfaction and joy of doing something commendable [in itself alone] without [resorting to] boastful comparison with his neighbor.
GALATIANS 6:3–4 AMPC

Lord, too often I find myself comparing my work with that of others. And then I find myself in one of two places: I'm either not satisfied or too satisfied with what I've accomplished. If it's the former, I begin to feel less worthy, less able, less competent. In other words, I feel less than who You've made me to be. If it's the latter, I find myself feeling too worthy, too capable, and too self-sufficient. Then before I know it, pride has set in. Help me, Lord, to find that middle ground. To know that my joy lies in comparing myself with myself and in doing my work for and in You. That is my reward. In Jesus' name, amen.

Day 336

THE MORNING STAR RISES

We have the prophetic word. . . . You will do well to pay
close attention to it as to a lamp shining in a dismal
(squalid and dark) place, until the day breaks through
[the gloom] and the Morning Star rises (comes into being)
in your hearts. . . . I waited patiently and expectantly
for the Lord. . . . [She proudly said] I am my beloved's,
and his desire is toward me! . . . Come, my beloved!
2 Peter 1:19; Psalm 40:1; Song of Solomon 7:10–11 ampc

Be with me, Lord Jesus, as I enter Your Word. Help me not just to read it but to take it in, absorb it, and allow it to work its way into my life. Let the light and power of Your Word break through the gloom within me until You rise up and come into being within my heart, changing whatever sorrows that linger into joy. You are my bright morning star, Jesus. I patiently wait for You. It is Your presence I expect to change me from the inside out, letter by letter, word by word. You are my beloved. Desire me as I desire You. Come, Jesus; come now. Amen.

Day 337
LIVING THE GOOD LIFE

And remember that the heavenly Father to whom you pray has no favorites. He will judge or reward you according to what you do. So you must live in reverent fear of him during your time here as "temporary residents." For you know that God paid a ransom to save you from the empty life you inherited from your ancestors. And it was not paid with mere gold or silver, which lose their value. It was the precious blood of Christ.
1 PETER 1:17–19 NLT

Heavenly Father, You ransomed me from an empty life through the precious blood of Your Son, Jesus. I owe You big-time for Your extravagant grace. My debt to You is unfathomable. But You didn't buy me from death to enslave me. You paid my price out of pure love. Because of that, I serve You for the sheer joy of pleasing You. You reward Your faithful followers in this temporary life. When I am beaten down from the struggle, remind me that this life is a pinprick in time. But what I do with this speck of time will impact my eternity. I long to hear "Well done, my good and faithful child" when I see You face-to-face. Amen.

Day 338
QUIET TIME

"The Lord is in His holy house. Let all the earth be quiet before Him." . . . He who is careful in what he says has much learning, and he who has a quiet spirit is a man of understanding. Even a fool, when he keeps quiet, is thought to be wise. When he closes his lips, he is thought of as a man of understanding. . . . O Lord, put a watch over my mouth. Keep watch over the door of my lips. . . . "Teach me, and I will be quiet. Show me where I have been wrong."
HABAKKUK 2:20; PROVERBS 17:27–28; PSALM 141:3; JOB 6:24 NLV

So often, Lord, the time I spend in Your presence is perhaps not really prayer. Lately, it's been a time during which I pour out my heart and mind to You, then go on my way, do my own thing. No wonder peace has been so elusive for me lately. So, help me, Lord, to stop my mental chattering. Pull me close. Let me rest my head against Your chest while I wait, still and silent. Tell me, Lord, what You have to say. Teach me what You'd have me know. Show me what You'd have me see in this quiet time with You. Amen.

Day 339
SPROUTING WITH HOPE

*He changes a desert into a pool of water and makes water
flow out of dry ground. And He makes the hungry go
there. . . . They plant seeds in the fields and plant grape-
vines and gather much fruit. He lets good come to them
and they become many in number. . . . He lifts those in
need out of their troubles. He makes their families grow
like flocks. Those who are right see it and are glad.*
PSALM 107:35–38, 41–42 NLV

When I'm in a place that seems dry of hope, Lord, I pray to
You, and You make water appear out of nowhere. Soon that
once-barren landscape within begins to come back to life. You
open my eyes to what may be. You urge me to plant seeds of
confidence and expectation in You. And soon I'm bearing more
fruit than I ever hoped or imagined. Good things begin to sprout
up, feeding every part of me—mind, body, spirit, and soul. Once
again, Lord, You lift me up out of myself and into You. And I am
overcome with gladness, singing with joy. Thank You, Lord, for
bringing me back to where You want me to be—joyfully expectant in You. Amen.

Day 340
TRUE HAPPINESS

Then Haman went out that day glad and with joy in his heart. But when he saw Mordecai at the king's gate, and when he did not stand up or show any fear in front of him, Haman was filled with anger. . . . For the Jews it was a time of joy and happiness and honor. In every part of the nation and in every city where the king's law had come, there was happiness and joy for the Jews.
ESTHER 5:9; 8:16–17 NLV

It's interesting, Lord, how I need to be sure of my source of joy. Does the joy I find in my life come from the deep well of knowing You, seeking You, and abiding in You? Or does my joy come from the shallow stream that eddies around my self-pride, honor, and worldly ambitions? The test seems to be that if my joy comes from the deep well of pleasing You instead of the shallow well of pleasing myself and the world, my happiness will not be fleeting but a deep, constant, and abiding joy. Help me seek my joy and happiness in You alone, Lord. For then I will find the everlasting gladness that comes only by living for and in You. Amen.

Day 341
NEVER TOO FAR

And God raised us up with Christ. . .in order that in the coming ages he might show the incomparable riches of his grace, expressed in his kindness to us in Christ Jesus. For it is by grace you have been saved, through faith—and this is not from yourselves, it is the gift of God—not by works, so that no one can boast.
EPHESIANS 2:6-9

God, I can never outrun Your grace or reach the border of Your mercy. Just when I think I've gone too far, reached a limit where Your grace cannot extend, I find Your love and mercy there too. No matter what I've done, no matter how dirty Satan tries to convince me I've become, You can raise me to new life in Christ and wash clean my stains. Because it's not about the things I've done; it's about who You are as the merciful God of heaven and earth. You've gifted me with extravagant grace I could never afford. My feeble attempts to please You could never purchase such a priceless treasure. Yet You give it away freely. In Jesus' name, amen.

Day 342

JUST WHEN YOU NEED IT

We do not have a High Priest Who is unable to understand and sympathize and have a shared feeling with our weaknesses and infirmities. . . . Let us then fearlessly and confidently and boldly draw near to the throne of grace (the throne of God's unmerited favor to us sinners), that we may receive mercy [for our failures] and find grace to help in good time for every need [appropriate help and well-timed help, coming just when we need it].
HEBREWS 4:15–16 AMPC

You, Jesus, know everything about me—my strengths and weaknesses, my ups and downs, my wins and losses, my solutions and problems. And You are more than familiar with all the hurts and hallelujahs that come into one's life. For You were mocked, betrayed, scorned, lashed, and tortured. Yet You still held Your peace. No matter what. That's the peace I want to have, Lord. As I draw near to You today, Lord, as I approach Your throne, please give me Your help, mercy, grace, and peace just when I need it. In Your name, amen.

Day 343
ALL MY TOMORROWS

Deceit is in the heart of those who devise evil, but those who plan peace have joy. . . . Anxiety in a man's heart weighs him down, but a good word makes him glad.
PROVERBS 12:20, 25 ESV

You, Lord, are a planner. You know exactly how everything is going to work out for me. Many times I've wished I knew what was going to happen. Yet at other times, I'm glad I cannot see into my future. Regardless of how I feel about knowing or not knowing, You've hidden my tomorrows from me. And as I walk this earth, I'm trusting that You will continue to be with me, for me, and in me. That You will forever be with me, loving and protecting me till the end of time. Because I trust You, I can rest in You. I can put all my tomorrows in Your hands. That leaves me free to plan peace. To find ways that I can becalm others. So plant some good words in my head, Lord. Then tell me who to speak them to so I can plant the peace and spread the joy I find in You. Amen.

Day 344

CONSTANT CONVERSATION

*Many, O Lord my God, are the wonderful works which
You have done, and Your thoughts toward us; no one
can compare with You! If I should declare and speak of
them, they are too many to be numbered. . . . I delight
to do Your will, O my God; yes, Your law is within my
heart. . . . Let all those that seek and require You rejoice
and be glad in You. . . . You are my Help and my Deliverer.*
PSALM 40:5, 8, 16–17 AMPC

I don't just want You, Lord, but I seek You out, wherever I am,
whatever I'm doing. I'm in constant conversation with You because I need You more than anything else in this world and the
next. There is no greater guide than You. No greater power,
force, refuge, strengthener. You don't just help me, Lord; You
deliver me. You get me out of so many sticky situations, often
ones I myself have made. Make me ever more aware of Your
presence and my need for You, Lord. In You I find all the joy I
could ever hope for or imagine. In Jesus' name, amen.

Day 345
I AM ACCEPTED

"Those the Father has given me will come to me, and I will never reject them. For I have come down from heaven to do the will of God who sent me, not to do my own will. And this is the will of God, that I should not lose even one of all those he has given me, but that I should raise them up at the last day."
JOHN 6:37–39 NLT

Father in heaven, I don't have to hide my flaws and failures or clean myself up to come to You. I can come as I am with no fear that You will reject me, because You came for the humble at heart. I've been cast aside by others, and it hurts. Their callous indifference threatened to strip me of my worth. But then I heard Your voice. You said, "Come." And Your forgiveness is available to anyone who asks. Your infinite grace covers all. You love me and welcome me because You created me. As a loving Father, You fold me in Your arms. When You return, You will raise me to new life with a glorious new resurrection body. In Jesus' name, amen.

Day 346
MIRRORING GOD'S TRANQUILITY

Every man to whom God has given riches and possessions, and the power to enjoy them and to accept his appointed lot and to rejoice in his toil—this is the gift of God [to him]. For he shall not much remember [seriously] the days of his life, because God [Himself] answers and corresponds to the joy of his heart [the tranquillity of God is mirrored in him].
ECCLESIASTES 5:19–20 AMPC

Too often, Lord, I find that the bad things that are happening in this world are overshadowing the blessings You have given me. That's put me in a very discontented state. That means I need to change my focus and attitude, Lord—and I need to do that right now. But I cannot do so without Your help. Lord, I want to do more than just focus on the blessings, all the riches and possessions You've given me, as well as the joys of working in and for You. What I desire even more, Lord, is to mirror Jesus. To nourish the peace and joy I have in You all the days of my life. In Jesus' name, amen.

Day 347
POWER OF THE WORD

*"The rain and snow come down from heaven and do
not return there without giving water to the earth. This
makes plants grow on the earth, and gives seeds to the
planter and bread to the eater. So My Word which goes
from My mouth will not return to Me empty. It will do
what I want it to do, and will carry out My plan well.
You will go out with joy, and be led out in peace."*
Isaiah 55:10–12 NLV

The power of Your Word, Lord, is astounding. Just as the rain
and snow You send to earth promote growth to the fields and
food to the farmer, so does Your Word provide growth and sus-
tenance in my life. It is food for my soul and water for my spirit.
Your Word carries out Your plan for me and all Your children.
Your promises, so much stronger than my good intentions, grow
me into the person You want and *need* me to be so that Your will
on earth will be done. And because of all this, I am on the path
of Your joy, led by Your peace. In Jesus' name, amen!

Day 348
PROTECTING ANGELS

He who dwells in the secret place of the Most High
shall remain stable and fixed under the shadow of the
Almighty [Whose power no foe can withstand]. I will say
of the Lord, He is my Refuge and my Fortress, my God;
on Him I lean and rely, and in Him I [confidently] trust! . . .
He will cover you. . . . You shall not be afraid. . . .
He will give His angels [especial] charge over you.
PSALM 91:1–2, 4–5, 11 AMPC

When I'm not trusting You, Lord, worry and dread take all the joy out of my life. So when I'm in that dark place of fretting and fearing, lift me up to that secret place—Your presence. Only there will I find the safety and courage I need! For when I'm in that place, no one—within or without—can withstand Your power. Lord, my refuge and fortress, on You alone I'm leaning and relying. In You I'm putting all my trust. In You alone do I gain the strength and courage I need to face the day and find the joy that comes from knowing Your angels are watching over me. So be it—amen!

Day 349
THE DAY IS NEAR

And do this, understanding the present time: The hour has already come for you to wake up from your slumber, because our salvation is nearer now than when we first believed. The night is nearly over; the day is almost here. So let us put aside the deeds of darkness and put on the armor of light.
ROMANS 13:11–12

Heavenly Father, with each passing day, I'm closer to eternity. You're putting the finishing touches on the home You have built for us in heaven, and I don't want to waste a minute of the time I'm given here. Keep me from becoming distracted with my day-to-day earthly life, and wake me up to what You are doing around me. I want to participate in Your good work. I want to cast off all my sin and put on Jesus. Don't allow me to be numbed by pleasure and comfort or to go grasping after everything I can get in this temporary life. Keep my eyes focused on eternity, for time is short. In the name of Jesus, amen.

Day 350
A HANDFUL OF QUIETNESS

I saw that all toil and all skill in work come from a man's envy of his neighbor. This also is vanity and a striving after wind. The fool folds his hands and eats his own flesh. Better is a handful of quietness than two hands full of toil and a striving after wind.
ECCLESIASTES 4:4–6 ESV

Trying to keep up with the Joneses is exhausting, Lord, and can go on forever. And that's not what I want to spend my life doing, for there's no peace to be found in such a competition. I'd much rather be working for You and striving for the things You want me to reach for, things such as peace, courage, patience, love, forgiveness, and compassion. So help me, Lord, to strike a balance between using my hands to meet the needs of the flesh and the needs of the spirit. And as I do so, Lord, help me to be more content with a handful of quietness in Your presence than clutching all the work I can handle with my only gain afterward being a fleeting pleasure soon blown away with the wind. Amen.

Day 351
CHANGE OF PLANS

*Do not always be thinking about your own plans only.
Be happy to know what other people are doing. Think as
Christ Jesus thought. Jesus has always been as God is. But He
did not hold to His rights as God. He put aside everything that
belonged to Him and made Himself the same as a servant who
is owned by someone. . . . He gave up His important place.*
PHILIPPIANS 2:4–8 NLV

Sometimes, Lord, I tend to get so wrapped up in my own life and plans that I never look around or show any interest in what's happening in the lives of others. Help me to reach out, Lord. I actually want to listen to the plans, dreams, and callings in the lives of others. Help me to put aside what I'd planned for today, even if it's just for a little while, and show an interest in another's ideas. And especially help me, Lord, to be more gracious amid interruptions, recognizing them not as something keeping me from getting what *I* want done that day but as opportunities to do what *You* would have me do to serve You. In Jesus' name, amen.

Day 352
A Story to Glory

What a beautiful thing, God, to give thanks, to sing an anthem to you, the High God! To announce your love each daybreak, sing your faithful presence all through the night. . . . You made me so happy, God. I saw your work and I shouted for joy. . . . My ears are filled with the sounds of promise: "Good people will prosper. . . . They'll grow tall in the presence of God, lithe and green, virile still in old age."
PSALM 92:1–2, 4, 11–14 MSG

When the world tries to drag me down into hopelessness, I'm going to fight back. I'm going to give thanks to You, Lord. I'm going to sing Your praises and proclaim how much You love me. I'm going to keep You with me throughout the day and then sing about how faithful You are to me at night. All my joy and happiness are bound up in Your promises and presence. As I look around me and see all the wonders You have created, I'll shout for joy. I'll revel in wonder. I'll grow tall in Your garden and continue to be productive, even when I'm old. May I be a story reflecting Your glory. In Jesus' name, amen.

Day 353
GETTING ALONG

Work at getting along with each other and with God.
Otherwise you'll never get so much as a glimpse of God.
Make sure no one gets left out of God's generosity. Keep
a sharp eye out for weeds of bitter discontent. A thistle
or two gone to seed can ruin a whole garden in no time.
Watch out for the Esau syndrome: trading away God's
lifelong gift in order to satisfy a short-term appetite.
HEBREWS 12:14–16 MSG

Lord, I want to live a life where I not only get along with people but go the extra mile to help them. You emphasize that I am to love You with all I am and love others as I love myself. You have created love to be Your children's pathway to peace. And that's the road I want to be on. But some people, Lord, are a bit hard to love. So please fill my heart with love, my soul with peace, and my lips with encouraging words as I reach out to all around me, in honor of Your Son, Jesus. Amen.

Day 354
EVERY HOUR

*And then he prayed, "God, I'm asking for two things
before I die; don't refuse me—Banish lies from my lips
and liars from my presence. Give me enough food to live
on, neither too much nor too little. If I'm too full, I might
get independent, saying, 'God? Who needs him?' If I'm
poor, I might steal and dishonor the name of my God."*
PROVERBS 30:7–9 MSG

You know the needs I have, Lord, as well as my desires to be
worry-free, to acquire a gentle and peaceful mien. To that end,
Lord, keep me honest at the core, and help me see beyond the
lies of others. Wherever needed, Lord, unveil the truth so that
I can find my way through this maze of life on earth. Yet also,
Lord, I ask for enough food to live on each day. Not too much
and not too little. Just enough to be nourished but not so much
that I get cocky and determine I don't need You anymore. For
the truth is, Lord, that I need You. Every hour. From now until
eternity. Amen.

Day 355
SHORE OF GOD'S DESIRE

When they had rowed three or four miles, they saw Jesus walking on the sea and approaching the boat. And they were afraid (terrified). But Jesus said to them, It is I; be not afraid! [I Aᴍ; stop being frightened!] Then they were quite willing and glad for Him to come into the boat. And now the boat went at once to the land they had steered toward. [And immediately they reached the shore toward which they had been slowly making their way.]
Jᴏʜɴ 6:19–21 ᴀᴍᴘᴄ

I thank You, Jesus, for always watching out for me. For coming into my life with all Your supernatural strength, with the power You wield to calm the wind and waves that threaten me, within and without. Help me to see You more clearly, Jesus. To recognize You as the friend and water walker You are. And even more, Lord, make me not just *willing* but *glad* to let You into my boat. When I do, I know I will be heading the way You want me to go, taking the course Father God planned for me to take. And I will at last find myself reaching the shore of Your desire for me. In Your name, I pray, amen.

Day 356
SMALL BEGINNING, GREATER END

*If you will seek God diligently and make your supplication
to the Almighty, then, if you are pure and upright, surely
He will bestir Himself for you and make your righteous
dwelling prosperous again. And though your beginning was
small, yet your latter end would greatly increase. . . . Behold,
as surely as God will never uphold wrongdoers, He will
never cast away a blameless man. He will yet fill your
mouth with laughter. . .and your lips with joyful shouting.*
JOB 8:5–7, 20–21 AMPC

When things seem to be going badly, when nothing seems to be
going my way, Lord, I hang on to the hope that You will hear and
answer my prayer. Your Son has made me pure and blameless
in Your eyes. Your Son has paved the way so that when I seek
after You and lift my soul to You, You bend Your ear to my lips.
I believe, Lord, that You will not only move on my behalf but
make things better than they were before—in Your own time.
I believe, Lord, that You will never turn away but will erase my
tears. You, in Your love and compassion, will once again fill my
mouth with laughter and my lips with shouts of joy. In Jesus'
name, I pray, amen.

Day 357
TAKING IT IN

"Job, are you listening? Have you noticed all this? Stop in
your tracks! Take in God's miracle-wonders!" . . . I look up
at your macro-skies, dark and enormous, your handmade
sky-jewelry, moon and stars mounted in their settings.
JOB 37:14; PSALM 8:3 MSG

Today, Lord, I have discord within and without, and I'm not sure
why. There's really nothing I can put my finger on as the cause
of this unease, but the feeling is there nevertheless. So I'm going to follow Your wisdom, Lord, which begins by opening up not
just my mind but my ears. There's been so much chattering in my
mind, Lord, that it's no wonder I feel a bit disconnected at times.
So I'm looking to open my eyes as well to see what's around me.
I'm going to stop all activity—working, playing, thinking, dream-
ing—and take in and appreciate all the beauty You have created,
all the miracles You've wrought, all the universe You sustain, all
the love and light You pour upon me. In Jesus' name, amen.

Day 358
BY FAITH

*Now faith is the assurance (the confirmation, the title
deed) of the things [we] hope for, being the proof of
things [we] do not see and the conviction of their reality
[faith perceiving as real fact what is not revealed
to the senses]. . . . By faith we understand that the
worlds. . .were framed. . .by the word of God, so that what
we see was not made out of things which are visible.*
HEBREWS 11:1, 3 AMPC

When stress knocks on my door, I soon find my faith taking a walkabout. An instant later, my peace is running after it. Then I'm left feeling like a quivering bowl of lime gelatin, shaking with doubts and anxieties. Lord, this is not at all how You want me to live. So, Lord, fill me with Your presence as I slowly take this next breath and another and another. As I seek You within, Lord, reveal Yourself, Your light, Your warmth, Your love. Remind me that all is well. That You will never leave or forsake me. That all I hope for is already on its way to me through You, my Lord and Savior. My hope and stay. Amen.

Day 359
JOYFUL AND OBEDIENT

You must keep on working to show you have been saved from the punishment of sin. Be afraid that you may not please God. He is working in you. God is helping you obey Him. God is doing what He wants done in you. Be glad you can do the things you should be doing. Do all things without arguing and talking about how you wish you did not have to do them. In that way, you can prove yourselves to be without blame.
PHILIPPIANS 2:12–15 NLV

Some days I feel like one of the wandering Israelites, Lord. I'm moaning and groaning about all the things I don't want to do. Help me to look at all the blessings in my life instead of at all the seeming curses. I want to please You, Lord. And no one likes a whiner. Open my eyes to what You are doing within me. Help me not to give up on myself—or You—but to recognize that You are helping me follow the path You have purposefully put before me. Make me pliant to Your directions. I want to become the joyful and obedient child You desire, walking in Your way instead of pouting and protesting on the sidelines. In Jesus' name, amen.

Day 360

FROM DAWN TO DUSK

He spread a cloud for a covering, and fire to give light at night. They asked, and He brought them quails for meat. And He filled them with the bread of heaven. He opened the rock and water flowed out. It flowed in the desert like a river. . . . He remembered His holy Word. . . . He brought His people out with joy, His chosen ones with singing.
PSALM 105:39–43 NLV

When I need to hide, Lord, You protect me, covering me with a cloud. When I am walking in darkness, in the deep shadows of night, You provide a fire to give light. When I ask for food, when I thirst for water, You provide both in abundance. You remember Your promises and You keep Your word. All the ways You take care of me are more than I can fathom, Lord. Be with me once more this day, from the time I begin my work for You until the moment I lay down my head. Bring me through, Lord, with joy. May my last thoughts be songs of praise to You. In Jesus' name, amen.

Day 361

JESUS, CHAMPION OF MY FAITH

*Do you see what this means—all these pioneers who blazed
the way, all these veterans cheering us on? It means we'd
better get on with it. Strip down, start running—and never
quit! No extra spiritual fat, no parasitic sins. Keep your eyes
on Jesus, who both began and finished this race we're in.
Study how he did it. Because he never lost sight of where
he was headed—that exhilarating finish in and with God.*
HEBREWS 12:1–2 MSG

Lord, I can envision it now. My days in this earthly life have ended, and I'm walking up the golden streets of heaven toward Your glorious throne. Crowds swell along the road, and they're cheering and celebrating—for me. I've run my race well. I followed Jesus, who showed me how to keep my eye on eternity; I've overcome and endured; and I've reached my heart-pounding finish line. Jesus steps forward and hugs me hard. He pulls back, and He's smiling wide. I'm a joint heir with Him. My Father cups His palms around my face with kind eyes shining and says, "Well done, My daughter." Lord, make this my reality. Help me throw off sin, and train me to think of eternity. Amen.

Day 362
SWEET PEACE

Wherever you find jealousy and fighting, there will be trouble and every other kind of wrong-doing. But the wisdom that comes from heaven is first of all pure. Then it gives peace. It is gentle and willing to obey. It is full of loving-kindness and of doing good. It has no doubts and does not pretend to be something it is not. Those who plant seeds of peace will gather what is right and good.
JAMES 3:16–18 NLV

I need some pointers, Lord, on how to make good decisions. In the past, I have talked to family members, partners, coworkers, and friends about what I should do, where I should go, how I should serve. But I still feel so very lost, not quite sure where my true path is. Perhaps, Lord, I've been looking for advice in all the wrong places. Instead of asking my fellow humans, I should be asking You for advice. So here I am, Lord, looking for Your knowledge, for that perfect heavenly wisdom that not only gives me peace but prompts me to plant seeds of peace. Ah, sweet peace, free of fears and worries, is Your wisdom and way. Amen.

Day 363
STANDING ON THE SHORE

Simon Peter announced, "I'm going fishing." The rest of them replied, "We're going with you." They went out and got in the boat. They caught nothing that night. When the sun came up, Jesus was standing on the beach, but they didn't recognize him. . . . He said, "Throw the net off the right side of the boat and see what happens." They did what he said. All of a sudden there were so many fish in it, they weren't strong enough to pull it in.
JOHN 21:3–4, 6 MSG

When I'm restless, anxious, afraid, impatient, confused, or frustrated, Lord, I find myself automatically going back to something familiar, something from my old life that once brought me comfort, hoping to regain my peace. Yet I soon discover that whenever I attempt anything without You, I come up empty. No matter how hard or how long I try or how much help I have, my endeavor without You bears no fruit. But then You appear on the scene, standing on the shore. You see me floundering in the sea. You, who appear to me a stranger, yell instructions. I obey. And my efforts pay off big-time! That's when I realize it's *You* standing on the shore. *You* are my blessing. *You* are my peace. *You* are my bounty. Amen.

Day 364

GOOD THINGS

Some traveled through the desert wastes. They did not find a way. . . . Their souls became weak within them. Then they cried out to the Lord in their trouble. And He took them out of their suffering. He led them by a straight path. . . . He fills the thirsty soul. And He fills the hungry soul with good things. . . . Let them give Him gifts of thanks and tell of His works with songs of joy.
PSALM 107:4–7, 9, 22 NLV

So often, Lord, I find myself just wandering. I cannot find my way in, out, over, around, under, or through. And as I go on wandering, my soul grows weak within me. Then I look up. I cry to You, longing to see Your face. And You come quickly. You lift me up, turn me around, show me the right way to go. As I follow Your directions, I see glimpses of You out ahead of me, beckoning, encouraging, loving. And in the resting places, You quench my thirsty and hungering soul with good—all that I need to thrive, to continue on with You. It is for this and so much more that I sing a song of praise and joy to You, the God of my life. Amen.

Day 365
GRACIOUSLY BLESSED

*John testified about him when he shouted to the crowds,
"This is the one I was talking about when I said, 'Someone
is coming after me who is far greater than I am, for he
existed long before me.' " From his abundance we have
all received one gracious blessing after another.*
JOHN 1:15–16 NLT

God, complaining comes easier to me than recognizing the ways I have been blessed. My perspective desperately needs an overhaul. My focus is too often snagged on my problems and all the things that are less than what I desire. But I have realized that I need to adopt an attitude of thanksgiving. While I allow one small snag to steal my joy, I miss the blessings flooding into my life. If I breathe, I am alive even if my health is less than perfect. I have spiritual life in You. I have hope and peace and love through Christ. I have received mercy and grace. I am rich beyond measure in You! Open my eyes to the countless blessings I've been given. Amen.

Scripture Index

Old Testament

New Testament

NOTES

....

....

....

....

....

....

....

....

....

....

....

....

....

....

....

....

NOTES

....

....

....

....

....

....

....

....

....

....

....

....

....

....

....

....

NOTES

....

....

....

....

....

....

....

....

....

....

....

....

....

....

....

....

NOTES

....

....

....

....

....

....

....

....

....

....

....

....

....

....

....

....

NOTES

....

....

....

....

....

....

....

....

....

....

....

....

....

....

....

....